Decorative

PICTURE FRAMING

Decorative

PICTURE FRAMING

MOYRA BYFORD

MEREHURST

To William

First published 1996 by Merehurst Limited,
Ferry House, 51–57 Lacy Road, London, SW15 1PR

Copyright © Merehurst Limited 1996

ISBN 1-85391-460-6

A catalogue record of this book is available from the British Library.

Edited by **David Holloway**
Designed by **Lisa Tai**
Photography by **Tony Robbins** (pages 2, 7, 39, 41, 45, 47, 51, 55, 57, 61, 65, 67, 71, 73, 77, 79, 83, 85 and 89) and **Mark Gatehouse**
(pages 9–37, 40, 42–44, 48–50, 52–54, 58–60, 62–64, 68–70, 72, 74–76, 78, 80–82, 84, 86–88 and 91–93)
Illustrations by **King & King**

Typesetting by Servis Filmsetting Ltd
Colour separation and printing by Toppan, Singapore

Contents

INTRODUCTION 6

EQUIPMENT AND MATERIALS 8

BASIC FRAMING TECHNIQUES 18

BASIC DECORATIVE TECHNIQUES 28

PROJECTS 38

Sepia photograph of great-grandma 40

Shell mirror 43

Kitchen memo board 46

Print of Old Master 50

Print-room effect 53

Miniature beaded frames 56

Child's painting 60

Oil painting on board 63

Set of flower prints 66

Underwater fish 69

Five variations with metal leaf 72

Greetings card 75

Kitchen poster 78

Watercolour 81

Octagonal frame 84

Clown mirror 88

Suppliers 94

Index 95

Introduction

Everyone has things that they want to have framed, maybe a family heirloom, old photographs, the first paintings that children brought back from school or just some holiday mementoes. I think it is more personal and a lot more fun to frame these things yourself and, what is more, it is not necessary to be a technical expert to make and decorate the frames that are in this book.

I started framing about twenty-five years ago and in those days styles were still very conventional – the main idea being that frames should last. Nowadays, fashions have changed considerably with pictures being thought of as part of the decor of the room, almost becoming disposable. While I do not altogether agree with our new throw-away world, I have tried to put together a selection of projects in this book that not only show some of the traditional forms of presentation, but also give you some more exciting ways of showing things off that may not be quite so long lasting, but are great fun!

In this book, I have tried to describe both the 'traditional' methods of framing and some modern contemporary treatments. Oil paintings, for example, traditionally were, and still are, framed with wide mouldings without glass. This is not always easy, and for this book I have bent the rules a little and suggested another way of creating the same effect. Watercolours, on the other hand, are traditionally framed with a rather narrower moulding and a washlined mount so I have included a very classically framed watercolour for you.

There are many other reasons why pictures are framed. Framing will not only make the picture look better and more important, but will also protect it from dirt and damage, make it more portable and make it easier to hang it on the wall to create a focal point in a room.

There are also many things other than pictures that we want to preserve and display and framing them is the answer, even if they are of no intrinsic value. Once framing materials were mass produced in the 19th Century, the Victorians could afford to feel much the same as we do, and a humble greetings card with a mount and frame was just as popular then as it is now.

The idea of decorating mounts also became popular in the 19th Century, later to be dropped for a more austere and plain look. Another revived 19th Century craft was decorating the frame moulding with collage and relief work. We are so fortunate today because there are so many paints, dyes and stains available.

The big revolution in picture framing, however, has occurred in the last thirty years and is the availability of reasonably-priced hand-operated equipment for the home picture framer to use. There is now an enormous and almost overwhelming choice in this area for anyone who wants to make their own frames. I shall be showing you how to make a frame and cut a mount before we start on the projects, but if you do not want to have a go at this, you can get your local picture framer to cut your moulding pieces and your mounts, which leaves you just the fun of decorating. And, of course, you can decorate ready-made frames and mounts – or restored second-hand ones.

I hope that the sixteen projects I have chosen for this book not only guide you, but also inspire you to continue to frame more and more interesting objects.

Equipment and Materials

A lot of decorative picture framing can be done with normal tools or equipment. But for good results, one or two specialist items will need to be bought and you will want a warm well-lit place where you can work. Much of the equipment and materials you need can be bought from art shops and do-it-yourself stores, but for some of the more specialised things you may need to go to a picture framing supplier.

Equipment and materials

TO MAKE IT EASIER FOR YOU TO DECIDE HOW MUCH you want to do, I have divided this section into four parts – making and assembling frames, decorating frames, cutting mounts and decorating mounts. I appreciate that not everyone will want to learn how to cut up and join mouldings to make frames, but will prefer to go straight to the decoration stage. This is fine, just ask your local picture framers to cut the pieces for you and go ahead with the decorating. If you talk to them nicely, they may assemble the frame for you afterwards, or you may decide to invest in a clamp to do this yourself – which has the added bonus that you can also strengthen old frames. The choice is yours. Similarly with mounts, you can have them cut, or learn the art of mount cutting yourself before you start to express your individuality in the decoration. With this in mind, I have suggested basic kits for each section, which you would need for almost every framing project you tackle.

Making and assembling frames

The basic requirement for making a picture frame is to cut four pieces of picture frame moulding to the correct size with their ends cut at an angle of exactly 45° (known as a mitre) and then to join them together to form a perfect rectangle with square corners. Picture frame moulding is different from ordinary timber moulding as it has a square cut-out – the rebate – to hold the picture, glass, mount and backing board.

MITRE SAW

If you want to make your own frames – which, financially, is a very beneficial thing to do – you will need to purchase a good saw. A tenon saw and simple mitre block can be used to cut mitres, but will not give you a good enough cut to make the accurate corners necessary for picture framing. A far better tool is a **mitre saw** and

there is an excellent range of inexpensive ones available. The saw has a machined metal bed for supporting the moulding and a fine-toothed saw blade that can be swung from side to side and locked in position to give 45° angles in both directions, making beautiful smooth cuts which join together perfectly for the frame corners. It can also be used to cut other angles for multi-sided frames – see the project on page 84 – and fixed settings are provided for these angles as well as 45°. Be sure that you buy a saw that has a detachable blade which can be renewed when it becomes blunt; some mitre saws have a clamp for securing the moulding and some have a depth stop which helps for repetitive cutting.

CLAMPS

The band clamp is the simplest and cheapest type of clamp for holding a picture frame while it is being joined with adhesive. It has a roll of plastic webbing coiled within the main body which can be pulled out to the distance around your frame. One corner of the frame is held by the body of the clamp; the other corners are held in place with moulded plastic shapes through which the band threads. The band can be locked and then tightened by means of a knob on the clamp body which pulls the whole frame together.

ADHESIVES

I find that most proprietary brands of PVA-based wood adhesive are perfectly satisfactory for frame making, though I always use the belt and braces method of pinning frame corners as well as gluing them. Always remove excess adhesive with a cotton bud before it dries.

HAMMER

A small hammer is the best for putting in panel pins and other delicate jobs. Choose the type which has a round head on one side and a flat head on the other. You will also need a narrow nail punch for driving panel pins home without damaging the wood.

DIMENSIONS
Throughout the book I have given both metric (m, cm and mm) and imperial measurements (ft and in). Work with whichever you feel more comfortable, but don't mix them. Normally, I have given exact equivalents – such as 2.5cm (1in) – but where the imperial measurement is an alternative I have given it as 1.5cm (or ½in).

SMALL CRAFT KNIVES

A 'Stanley' type craft knife (preferably the retractable type) is indispensable in the picture framing workshop, but be sure to have plenty of spare blades. A scalpel is also very useful for precise work.

GLASS CUTTER

If you need to cut glass, the best glass cutters have an oil reservoir which dispenses a small amount of oil on to the glass every time pressure is applied. This makes cutting a lot easier.

MOULDINGS

You can buy an absolutely massive range of *finished* mouldings, but if you choose one of these you cannot usually decorate it further.

My own favourite mouldings are the plain, *unfinished*, timber mouldings now available. These are perfect for decoration and are available in ramin, oak, obeche or pine. Different effects can be obtained with the same dyes on different woods and so an infinite range of colours can be made. The other advantage of these mouldings is that you can avoid wastage by cutting the four pieces for a frame before colouring, leaving the remnant of the length of moulding to be stained a different colour for another frame. Most mouldings are sold in lengths from two to three metres (6ft 6in to 10ft), and once you have cut a frame from a finished moulding you can often be left with a virtually unusable piece which is not big enough for another whole frame.

When buying mouldings, you will need to know some of the words used to describe the main shapes. A

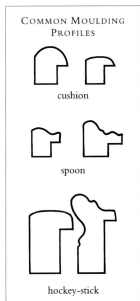

COMMON MOULDING
PROFILES

cushion

spoon

hockey-stick

flat moulding is what it says, whilst a **cushion** moulding has a gently curved front face. I like to use **hockey-stick** moulding which has a curved face, but a very deep rebate, and you will find a variety of ornately shaped mouldings known as **scoop** or **spoon**. One technical term you will come across is the 'sight-edge' – this is the part of the moulding (or the mountboard) closest to the picture. Sometimes, you will want to decorate this.

BACKING BOARDS

A picture is backed for protection and thick card, hardboard or MDF board can be used. Hardboard used for picture framing is smooth on both sides and yet only 2mm (³⁄₃₂in) thick, so it does not fill up too much space in the rebate. It can be bought in large sheets which will do for several pictures, or you may be able to buy smaller pieces from your local picture framers.

GLASS

Glass is used to protect watercolours, prints and other pictures with a mount, but oil paintings and acrylics are traditionally not glazed. Sometimes a coat of varnish will suffice for protection on items that will be short lived. If you need to use glass and feel unhappy about the idea of cutting it, your local glass retailer is quite used to cutting individual pieces. This may cost a little more, but you will save on sticking plasters! Make sure you ask for 2mm picture glass and never try to use old pieces of 3mm or 4mm window glass which will make the frame too heavy.

Basic Assembly Kit

1 *Glass cleaner*
2 *Bradawl*
3 *Gummed brown paper tape*
4 *Pushmate and tabs*
5 *Screw eyes*
6 *Masking tape*
7 *Nylon picture cord (medium thickness)*

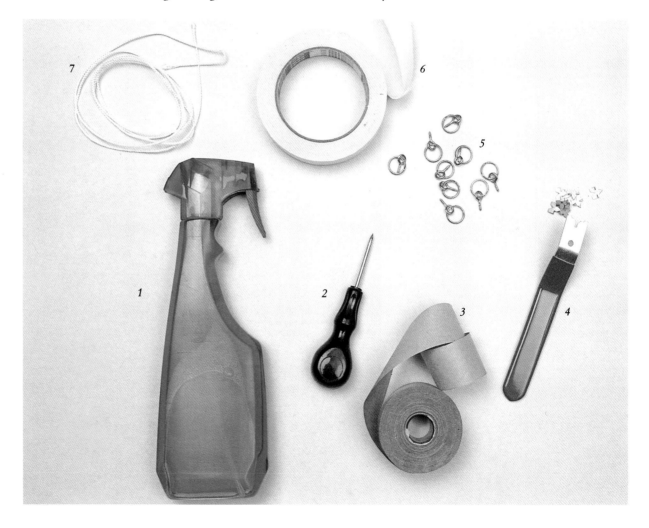

GLASS CLEANER

Just before the frame is assembled, you must clean the glass thoroughly. I find most types of spray-on clear glass cleaner perfectly adequate for this.

FASTENING DEVICES

The glass, mount, picture and backing board all need to be secured into the frame. The cheapest way to do this is with panel pins and a hammer (which, for most frames, you will need anyway for strengthening the corners), but it is a very difficult method and almost impossible to get a tight fit.

A 'pushmate' is a more sophisticated way of achieving the same result. This device pushes small shaped tabs into the inner sides of the frame to hold everything in place. Similar results can be achieved using a brad gun, which fires metal pieces into the frame.

TAPES

The backs of pictures are traditionally finished with gummed brown paper tape about 4cm (13½in) wide. This keeps out the dirt and makes a nice neat finish. Masking tape is useful for a variety of jobs and the most common width that I use is 2.5cm (1in).

NAILS, SCREW EYES AND HOOKS

The very thinnest panel pins are used to pin corners together, use 12mm (½in) pins for narrow mouldings and 25mm (1in) ones for wider mouldings.

Use a medium-weight screw eye for the hanging cord – some screw eyes have an additional ring which allows the cord to lie flatter. A bradawl is the best tool for starting the hole for a screw eye. Alternatively, for a small decorative frame, you can use an ornamental hanger screwed to the top of the frame at the back.

CORD VERSUS WIRE

I have always preferred to use nylon cord rather than picture wire to hang pictures as it is available in a range of thicknesses and is very durable. Do not attempt to hang a picture on cord that is too fine, or use string or any other unsuitable material.

Cutting mounts

You can cut a mount to size with a craft knife (used along the side of a suitable metal straight-edge), but one of the most important jobs in picture framing is cutting the bevelled-edge aperture in the mount which reveals the picture underneath.

HAND-HELD MOUNT CUTTER

For cutting a bevelled-edge aperture, the most basic piece of equipment that you can buy is a hand-held mount cutter, and you can do a lot of work with it before you feel the need to move to something more extravagant. Some people always cut their mounts with a hand-held cutter, and I certainly have one or two by me for small jobs in the studio.

There are many cutters on the market, but your choice should be determined by some basic factors. Hand-held cutters all depend on running the cutter along a line that you have previously drawn on your mountboard. It is therefore imperative that you choose a cutter which allows you to see the start and finish of the line that you have marked. Curiously, not all cutters allow you to do this, so it is a point to watch.

Some cutters have their own straight-edge which they hook on to and run along, and these are a little more expensive. Otherwise, the cutter has to run along a separate straight-edge which can be a little difficult to hold steady and this may influence your choice. Lastly, there is the choice of a fixed blade or a retractable blade. I find that I have no difficulty with either, but you may feel that a retractable blade is easier to manage.

If you are going to do a lot of mount cutting, it might be worth investing in a more sophisticated (and, of course, more expensive!) machine, which has the straight-edge attached to a board, which holds the mountboard firm. Some of these cutters have adjustable stops at the ends so that you do not have to mark out your mountboard, but some still require you to draw your rectangle with the crosses at the corners.

Some subjects require a circular or oval aperture to be cut in the mount. If you want to do this yourself, you really need to buy a circle or oval/circle mount cutter.

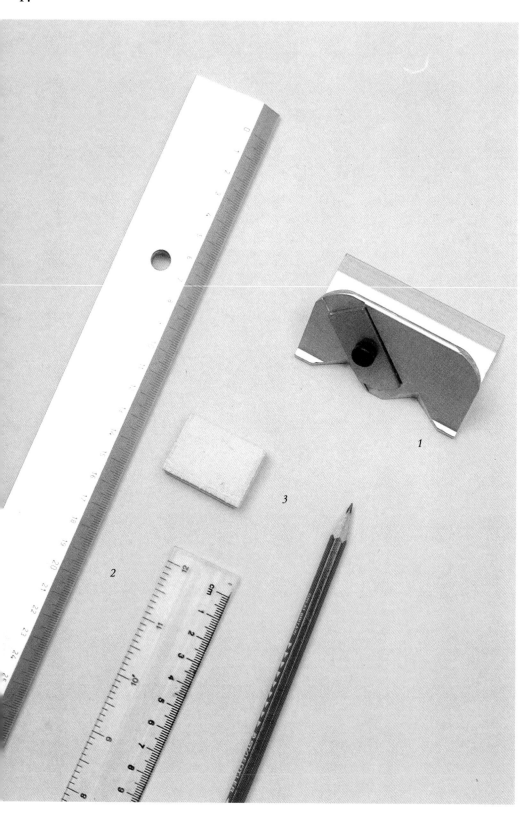

However, these are expensive and to start with you can buy mounts with ovals and circles already cut or ask your local picture framers to do the cutting for you.

STRAIGHT-EDGES AND RULERS

A good quality metal straight-edge of at least 50cm (or 18in) is essential if you intend to use a simple hand-held cutter. If you want to cut mounts from full-size sheets of mountboard you will need a straight-edge of 1m (or 3ft). In addition to this a 1m (or 3ft) clear plastic ruler with bevelled edges and marked in both centimetres and inches is invaluable.

MOUNTBOARD

There is an overwhelming selection of mountboard available in different colours (including gold and silver) and with different finishes (including cloud, flannel, textured and ingres as well as plain).

Mountboard comes in large sizes – 112 × 81.5cm (44 × 32in) – so each sheet can be cut into several mounts. It is therefore best to select neutral shades to start with to give you maximum versatility and avoid wastage. Some art shops and picture framers will sell half sheets, but these usually work out more expensive.

TAPES

Double-sided adhesive tape is used when fastening double mounts together and masking tape is used for holding the picture to the mount.

PENCILS AND RUBBERS

Mountboard marks very easily so clean hands are a must. A very sharp HB pencil used lightly is the only acceptable marker. Never use a ball-point pen on mountboard. Some dirty marks can be removed with a putty rubber which is obtainable in art shops.

Basic Mount Cutting Kit

1 *Hand-held mount cutter*
2 *Straight-edge and ruler*
3 *HB pencil and putty rubber*

Decorating frames

There are many ways in which you can decorate picture frames and most decoration – painting, staining, liming and waxing of the wood, for example – is carried out on the moulding after it has been cut, but before it is joined. This makes it easier to get an even coating.

BRUSHES AND SPONGES

I use best quality narrow household painting brushes for painting frames as I find that the natural bristles withstand both oil and acrylic paint and last well. Be careful of cheap brushes as they will tend to lose their bristles. You will also need some artist's brushes for finer decora-tion and touching up. You can try both natural and synthetic sponges for decoration as they will give different effects. I always feel that natural sponges should give the best results – but then end up using a small piece cut off a synthetic sponge!

WOOD DYES

There is an excellent range of water-based wood dyes that have been developed to use with plain unfinished mouldings. They come in two ranges – pastel colours and natural wood colours. Spirit-based wood dyes produce a very strong, hard colour and are available in a small basic range of shades.

Basic Frame Decorating Kit
(These items can be bought gradually)
1 *Small cans of wood dyes*
2 *Paints*
3 *Collection of sponges*
4 *Self-hardening modelling clay*
5 *Liming wax and a selection of other waxes*
6 *Artist's brushes*
New narrow household painting brushes (not shown)

PAINTS

The new artists' paints are excellent for decorating mouldings. They can be mixed to produce a solid opaque effect or diluted with water to produce a more translucent finish. I also use small sample ('tester') pots of household acrylic paint and I like to have a selection of small tins of gloss paint – the basic colours of red, green, blue, yellow, white and black are the most useful.

Have a look in art shops for gold paints. Most makes come in different shades of gold and it is a good idea to have several on hand to link with golds on finished mouldings and also with gold mountboard.

WAXES

My favourite wax has to be liming wax which is very effective when used on a strong grained wood such as oak. It seems a wasteful sort of process because it is worked into the wood and then almost immediately rubbed off again, but a small amount is left in the grain and the effect is quite miraculous. Wood-coloured waxes are also very useful for adding depth of colour. Similarly gold waxes can be used to add a little shimmer to a colour.

METAL LEAF

An effective way of decorating a frame is with metal leaf, which can be used either on bare wood or on stained or painted wood. It is attached by means of gold size which is painted on. Metal leaf is very cheap and comes on a roll of approx. 3 – 4cm (1¼ – 1½in) wide backed on paper. It is not easy to handle, however, and to start with I would advise using it in small patches.

MODELLING CLAY

I use a brand of self-hardening modelling clay when I want to build up a frame to produce a relief effect. This is very easy to work, yet sets hard and can be sanded if necessary. I also use it if I want to attach things such as shells to a frame and it makes a very good filler. Alternatively, a proprietary brand of ceramic tile adhesive is useful for attaching things to frames and has the advantage of being pure white.

Decorating mounts

I feel that mount decoration is one of the most exciting parts of picture framing as it allows you to add a very personal touch to the whole picture.

CORNER GAUGE

The most essential piece of equipment for decorating mounts is a graduated corner gauge. This is a piece of clear plastic with a short ruler or a right angle which tucks neatly into the corner of the bevelled-edge aperture in the mount to allow you to measure and mark across the mount at the corners.

PENS

The most sophisticated pen is an artist's ruling pen. This is stainless steel and the distance between the two parts of the tip can be adjusted with a thumbscrew to alter the width of line. The pen is loaded with paint and care must be taken to put sufficient paint into it to complete a line without putting so much paint in that it blots. With practice, this pen will become your best friend.

Some fibre-tipped pens can be used for drawing lines on a mount, but they should be capable of a very fine and crisp line. Nothing is worse than lines drawn round a mount with a child's garish felt-tip pen. Gold and silver fibre-tip pens are, however, very effective and are a good stand-by in the workshop.

BRUSHES AND SPONGES

Only the very best artist's sable brushes should be used for decorating mounts. For free-hand decoration you will need the usual pointed round brushes in a selection of sizes. For washlining, you will need a good quality flat brush, the size I use most is 13mm (½in). A selection of sponges is useful, particularly a new synthetic bath sponge which can be cut into shaped pieces.

OTHER BITS AND PIECES

White paper kitchen roll, cotton wool, cotton buds and scraps of card can all be used to decorate mounts. A child's airbrush (used with its coloured felt-tip pens) and spray bottles are also useful.

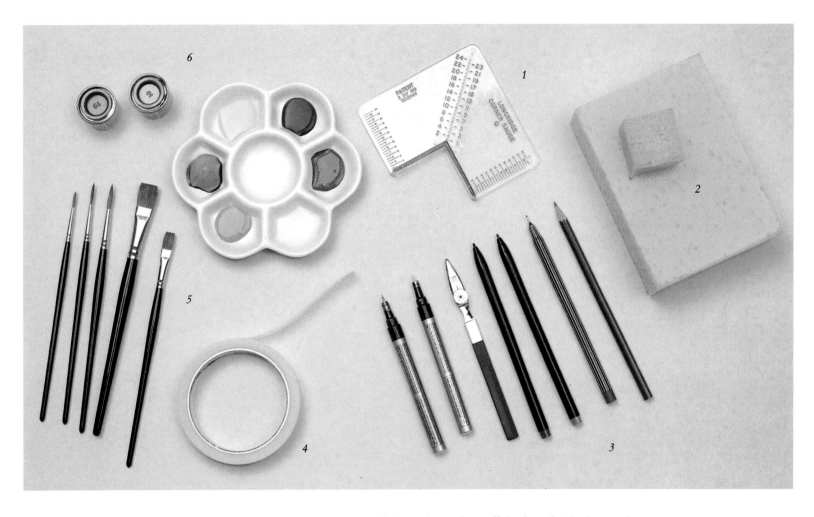

SELF-ADHESIVE DECORATIONS

Rolls of printed borders are available to apply to a mount for a very quick, instant effect. This is cheating, but in some instances they can look very effective and it is good to know how to apply them – see the *Print of Old Master* project on page 50.

You can also get sheets of self-adhesive corners and flourishes which, when used sparingly, can look very good. Lastly, there is self-adhesive lettering, which is applied rather laboriously letter by letter, but is very useful if you need to make a title and are not enough of a calligrapher to print the letters yourself.

TAPES

The only tape that you dare to apply to the **face** of a mountboard is magic finger-lift tape; any other type of

tape will drag the surface off the board. Magic tape is marvellous for creating a mask so that you can make a decorative border, and a roll of it is essential equipment for any mount decorator. You can also obtain sheets of low-tack masking film for making stencils.

PAINTS

I use the new type of artists' paints extensively in mount decoration as they are so versatile. They can be applied thickly straight from the pot, or diluted to form a water-colour. In a slightly diluted state they are excellent in a ruling pen for ruling lines.

Artists' watercolours can also be used in mount deco-ration. Free-hand decorations are fine with pan or tube water colours, but I prefer the liquid water colours for spraying as there is no danger of lumps.

Basic Mount Decorating Kit

1 *Corner gauge*

2 *Selection of sponges*

3 *Pencil, fibre-tipped pens, ruling pen, gold and silver pens*

4 *Magic or finger-lift tape*

5 *Sable artist's brushes (Nos 1, 3 and 5) and flat brushes (½in and ¼in – 12mm/6mm)*

6 *Paints, either a set of the new artists' paints or watercolours*

Basic Framing Techniques

When you start framing and mount cutting, you will need some off-cuts of moulding and pieces of mountboard to practice on. My local picture framing shop often has these for sale very cheaply, and they are absolutely ideal to learn with. They can be made into small frames that can then be used for things like photographs and will give you practice without too much expense.

B a s i c   f r a m i n g   t e c h n i q u e s

A GOOD 'PRACTICE' FRAME TO MAKE IS 20 BY 15CM (OR 8 by 6in), which can later be used with or without a mount for framing standard-sized photographs.

USING THE MITRE SAW

To cut the frame moulding, start by swinging the saw blade to the left and lock it in the 45° position. Lift the saw blade gently in your right hand, place the end of the moulding underneath it with the rebate facing you and gently lower the blade on to the moulding. Hold the moulding firmly with your left hand pressing it down and against the back of the saw bed. Draw the handle towards you for the first cut, then saw gently and evenly all the way through the moulding.

The measurement for the frame is taken on the inside of the rebate and a small allowance of 2mm (or 1/16in) is added to the measurement for 'ease' so that the glass, mount and backing will slip into the finished frame easily. For your 'practice' frame mark 20.2cm (or 8 1/16in), the measurement for the long side of the frame, on the inside edge of the rebate and then continue the line round on to the top of the moulding above the back of the rebate. Swing the saw blade to the right and lock it in position. Lift the blade and insert the moulding, positioning it so that the cut will cross your mark. Cut as before. This is now your master piece which you can use to measure the other long side – or, if you are making a set of frames the same size.

▶ *To make the first cut with the mitre saw, swing the blade to the left and cut off the end of the moulding with the rebate facing you.*

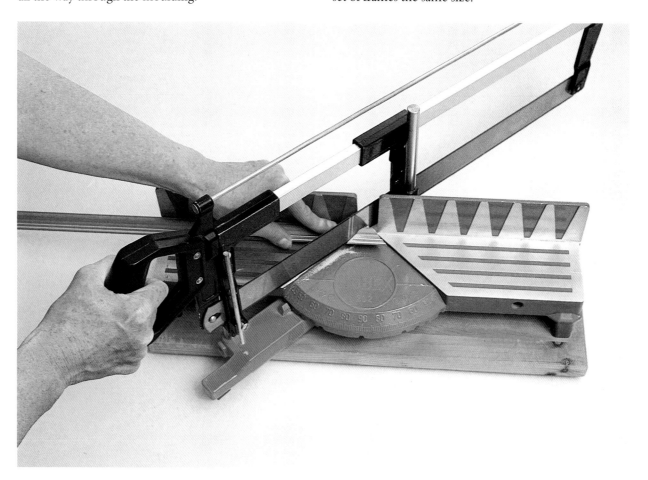

To cut the second piece of this length make the preliminary cut with the saw blade on the left-hand side, then put the length of moulding back to back with the master to mark the required length on the back. Move the blade to the right and make the second cut.

Repeat this whole process for the two short sides of the frame – in this instance, making these 15.2cm (or 6 ⅛in) long. Always cut the long sides of any frame first – if you make a mistake on one, it can be cut down to make a short side!

READY-MADE FRAMES

Widely available, these are a good quick alternative for use around a decorated mount. They are normally sold complete with glass, but in my experience the backing boards provided are not of the quality of 2mm hardboard and so may need substituting.

GLUING AND CLAMPING

The four pieces of moulding are now put into a band clamp. Release the lock on the clamp and draw the band out to roughly the shape of the frame, slotting it through the three corner pieces. Adjust the clamp and the four lengths of moulding until everything is square. Remove the two short lengths and spread wood adhesive sparingly on both ends so that all four corners will be glued. Replace and then tighten the band slightly and lock in position checking that the four corners are square and the whole frame is straight, and start to apply pressure by tightening. The adhesive will be squeezed out of the joints and should be wiped away with a cotton bud so that you can see whether the corners are still positioned correctly. Continue tightening until the band is twanging, remove any more excess adhesive and then leave two to three hours for the adhesive to set.

PINNING

For anything other than small lightweight frames, the corners should be reinforced with panel pins. With the frame held upright, hammer the pins in gently – a narrow nail punch can be used to drive the pin head

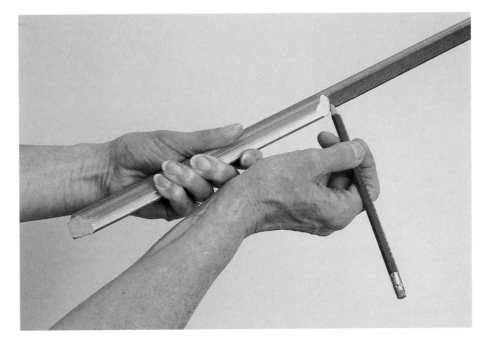

▲ *After transferring the frame measurement on to the moulding, swing the saw blade to the right, positioning* the moulding at the mark and make the second cut, again holding the moulding firmly in place.

▼ *Use the first cut length of moulding as a 'master' to mark the length of the opposite piece.*

► *To join the frame, position the mouldings in the clamp with plastic support pieces at each corner and apply adhesive to both ends of each short piece of moulding.*

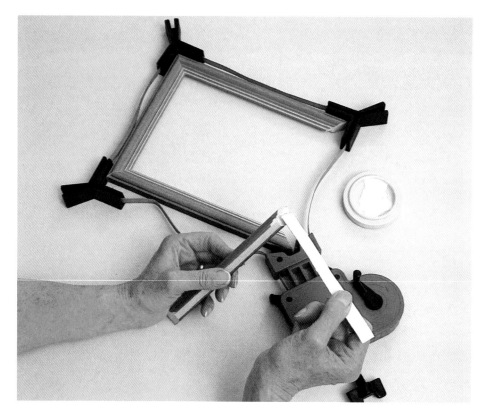

▼ *Lock the clamp, checking that each corner is square, and removing excess adhesive, then continue tightening the clamp and leave 2–3 hours until the adhesive has set.*

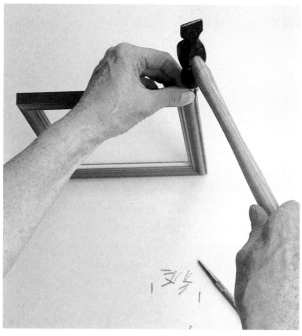

▲ *Stand the frame upright on a flat surface when hammering in reinforcing panel pins at the corners.*

below the surface and the tiny holes filled (and, if necessary, touched up with paint or stain) afterwards.

ASSEMBLY

The backing board, glass (and mount, if required) are all cut to the same measurement – for our 'practice' frame, this is 20 × 15cm (or 8 × 6in) – and they should slip into the frame easily as it has been cut fractionally bigger.

To cut the backing board – usually 2mm hardboard – first mark it out to size with a pencil and ruler and then score twice along the marked lines with a craft knife against a straight-edge. If you move the scored line to the edge of a table and 'crack' the board down and then up, you will find that it will break easily along the line. Any slightly rough edges can be sanded away. See page 25 for mount-cutting techniques.

If you are having your glass cut for you, take the frame along to the glass retailer so that it can be made exactly to the right size. If you want to have a go yourself, mark out the size with a felt-tip pen and use your glass cutter against a straight-edge to make one firm score. You will hear the scratch when the glass is being scored correctly. Place the scored line along the edge of a piece of board or over a matchstick and press down gently. The glass should break cleanly along the line. It is best to have some spare pieces of glass to practise on until you become confident.

To clean the glass, use a proprietary brand of glass cleaner and a soft cloth. Immediately the glass has been cleaned, put it in the frame followed by the mount, picture and finally the backing board. Do not delay in doing this or specks of dust will fall on the glass and you will have to start cleaning all over again. The backing board needs to be fastened firmly in place with either hammer and pins or a pushmate. The pins or securing tabs need to be about 8cm (or 3in) apart and spaced out evenly around the frame.

The back of the frame is then sealed against dirt and insects with gummed brown paper tape. Tear off four pieces of tape which are longer than the sides of the frame, damp one at a time on a wet sponge and place it neatly and evenly on the back of the frame covering the

join and slightly away from the edge. Tape two opposite sides first, then tape the other two sides allowing the tapes to cross at the corners. Put the frame somewhere flat to dry, which will take about an hour, then carefully trim the excess tape away. The back should now look neat as well as being properly sealed.

Screw eyes are placed roughly ⅓rd of the way down the side of the frame and in the centre of the underside of the moulding. Make a starter hole with a bradawl, then screw in the eye to the hilt by hand.

The hanging cord is threaded through the screw eyes and I always think it is best used double. The ends are

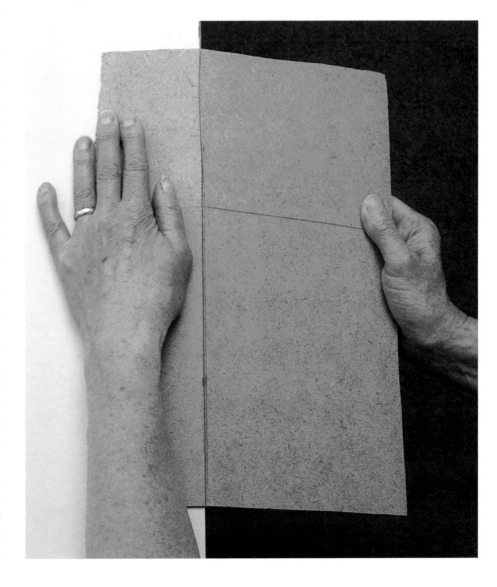

▼ *To cut hardboard, make a double score along the marked line and 'crack' it across a table edge. Use sandpaper to smooth the edges.*

▲ The glass, mount, picture and backing board can easily be secured into the frame using a pushmate and tabs.

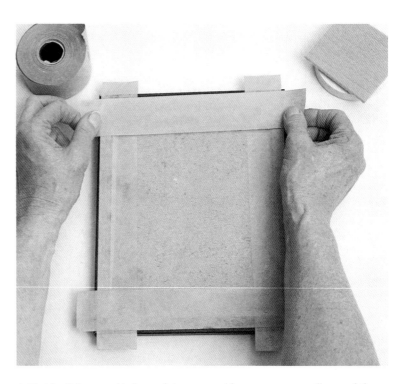

▲ Finish off the assembly by applying gummed brown paper tape all around the back to give a neat result.

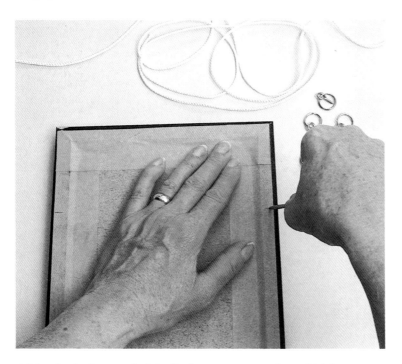

▲ Use a bradawl to start the holes for the screw eyes around one-third the way down from the top of the frame.

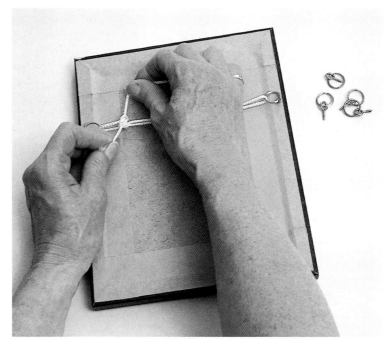

▲ Fix the hanging cord with the knot to one side so that it does not get in the way of the picture hook.

tied around both pieces of the cord and the knot is made to one side so that it does not interfere with the hook when the picture is hung.

MAKING FRAMES FROM OTHER MATERIALS

There is no need to use conventional mouldings to make a picture frame. Frames can equally well be made from a flat piece of wood (plywood is a good choice) with the appropriate size of hole cut in the middle to form an aperture. The wood can then be painted, stained or decorated as required. However, some arrangement has then to be made on the back to contain the glass, picture and backing board. I have shown such a frame in my *Miniature beaded frames* project on page 56 and *Kitchen poster* project on page 78.

Cheap frames can also be made from cardboard or corrugated paper, where maximum advantage can be taken of the lined effect. These frames do not last very well, however, and so are really suitable only for use with photographs or other 'temporary' pictures.

REJUVENATING OLD FRAMES

When I want an old frame, my first port of call is the local car boot sale. Quite good frames can be picked up cheaply and if you are lucky they have their glass and backing board intact, so everything can be recycled. Another good source of supply is the local saleroom or auction house. Try to go to a household sale rather than an antiques sale and you should find boxes of discarded frames amongst the various lots.

Sometimes the corners on old frames will be a little loose and need to be strengthened. Insert a little wood adhesive into the corners, put the frame into your band clamp, tighten the whole thing up and leave the adhesive to dry. To make sure that the corners of large frames are strong, hammer in a 50mm (2in) oval nail (with the long side along the grain) in each corner then cover the head with a little filler.

Most old wooden frames benefit from a rub over with fine wire wool. This will get rid of any dirt and grime and prepare the surface for painting. Do not, however, use wire wool on gilt frames.

CHOOSING MOUNT PROPORTIONS

The size of border you need on your mount depends partly on the size of picture you are framing and the effect you want to achieve – some small pictures, for example, can look good in a mount with narrow borders, whilst others might need a wider border. There are no rules about this, so take your time experimenting with mountboard offcuts until you get the effect you are happy with.

You will usually need wider borders when you want to add decoration to the mount – the amount you need for this depends on the type and size of the decorative effect. Once you have decided on the proportions of the mount, the mountboard has to be cut to size and then the bevelled-edge aperture made.

CUTTING MOUNTS TO SIZE

To cut a mount to size, first mark out the measurements on a large sheet or mountboard, trying to minimise any wastage. Place the sheet on a piece of spare backing board and cut through the mountboard firmly with a craft knife. For our 'practice' frame, the mount is 20cm by 15cm (or 8in by 6in).

▼ *Use fine wire wool to clean up an old frame.*

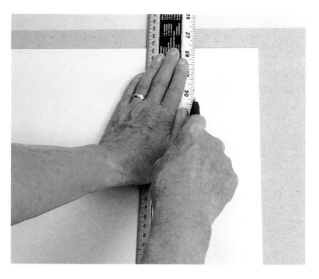

▲ *Cut mountboard to size on some spare backing board with a craft knife along a firmly held straight-edge.*

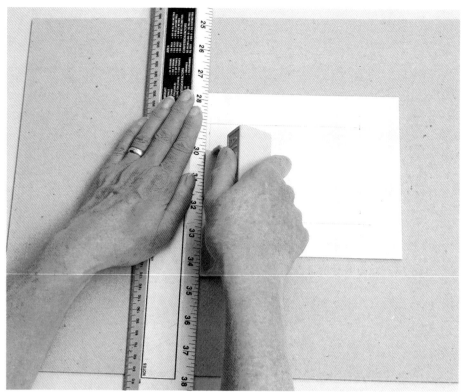

▶ *Once the size of the aperture has been marked out on the back of the mount, position your straight-edge correctly and use a hand-held mount cutter to cut the first bevel.*

▶ *After cutting round all four edges of the aperture (rotating the mount clockwise for each cut), the centre 'fall-out' should come away easily. If not, use a scalpel to remove it.*

CUTTING THE APERTURE

A good size of border for the mount to fit our 'practice' frame would be 3cm (1¼in). You can use the width of your ruler to mark this out – this time on the back of the mountboard – making lines parallel to the edge, adding 5mm (³⁄₁₆in) to the bottom border and crossing the lines at the corners.

Position your straight-edge and hand-held mount cutter parallel to the line so that, when inserted, the blade of the cutter will start at the cross and run along the line. When you are satisfied that you are in position, insert the blade and push along the line stopping at the cross at the other end. Take your blade out, turn the mount clockwise and reposition the cutter on the next side and repeat the process until all four sides are cut and the centre comes away: this is called the 'fall-out'. You will probably need to practise with your cutter for a little while to attain perfectly straight sides and crisp corners without overcuts. If you undercut a corner slightly, use a scalpel to remove the fall-out.

CUTTING A DOUBLE MOUNT

If two pieces of mountboard are cut to the same overall size, but given different widths of border, it is possible to get an interesting effect when they are placed together. Two different colours can be used, but two mounts of the same colour are also surprisingly effective. The two mounts are held together with double-sided adhesive tape. A small piece of tape is placed on each side of the lower mount called the 'inner', well back from the cut edge, the protective paper is peeled off and the 'outer' or top mount is carefully placed in position. Double-sided adhesive tape is very sticky so you have only one chance to get the position correct.

FASTENING A PRINT INTO A MOUNT

The simplest way of doing this is with masking tape. Lie the print face up on the table, slip two pieces of masking tape about 8cm (or 3in) long under the print diagonally across the top corners. Hold the mount over the print, in the correct position and gently lower it on to the print checking all the time that it is in the right place. When it is on the print, press firmly on the top corners and it should be held sufficiently for you to be able to turn the whole thing over. More tape can then be applied on the other sides if necessary.

◀ *A double mount allows you to have two borders of different widths in the same or in contrasting colours.*

▼ *To fasten a picture to its mount, place the picture face up on a surface with masking tape diagonally across the top corners and position and press down the mount exactly where you want it. Add more tape on the back of the picture if necessary.*

Basic Decorative Techniques

Decoration can be applied to the frame, to the mount or to both, depending on the picture that is being framed. There is obviously more scope for decoration when the frame is around something plain like a mirror, a memo board or even an old sepia photograph, but when decoration is going to be used with a painting or coloured print the whole effect must harmonise.

Decorating frames

ALL FRAMES ARE DYED AFTER THEY ARE CUT AND before they are assembled. This avoids the uneven effect that may occur if adhesive has been squeezed on to the surface of the moulding at the corners, which would have the effect of sealing the wood and preventing the dye from taking properly.

DYEING

I apply water-based dye with wads of cotton wool and wear rubber gloves. Pour a small amount of dye on to the cotton wool and apply it directly and evenly to the first moulding. Make sure that the edges and the back of the moulding are also covered. Repeat this on the other three pieces of moulding and leave to dry.

Exciting colour variations can be obtained by putting one dye over another, and a different effect is achieved when the second colour is applied before the first one has dried. You should therefore save all your offcuts so that you can experiment with them and find colour combinations that you like. For example if you are using rose and lavender dyes, apply the rose first then, while it is still wet, apply the lavender. Repeat, this time waiting until the rose dye is dry. This will produce two completely different colours – and if you put the lavender on first and then the rose, you can get two more colours.

Further experiments can be made with combinations of the pastel colours and the wood colours which produce a range of more subtle shades. The important thing to remember is that the colour that you finally select must link with and complement the picture and mount that will be in the frame.

Spirit-based dyes are very intense and should only be used when you need a hard bright colour. They can also be applied with cotton wool wads, but should be used sparingly, one coat usually being sufficient.

USING WAX

Liming wax is most effective when used on a strongly-grained wood such as oak and is particularly pleasing if it is applied after water based dyes, although it can be applied on bare wood. Allow the wood to dry completely if it has been dyed, then apply the liming wax liberally with a pad of wire wool, rubbing it into the grain of the wood. If you are liming a small or medium size frame, you can work the liming wax into all four pieces before you start to rub it off, but if you are working on a large frame, it is best to work on just two pieces at a time because the liming wax has to be rubbed off within a few minutes and should **never** be allowed to dry because it sets hard.

Clear wax and a soft cloth is used to rub the liming wax off and will simultaneously produce a very pleasant sheen on the wood. If your moulding has a sculptured profile it is very good to leave some liming wax in the grooves to accentuate the effect.

The colour of the wood (or the dyed wood) moulding can be changed by the application of coloured

▼ *The best way to apply dyes to wood moulding is with wads of cotton wool.*

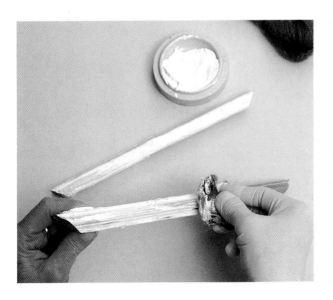

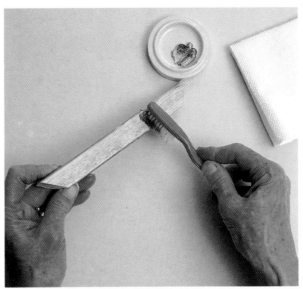

◀◀ *Liming wax is applied liberally to a plain or dyed moulding using wire wool.*

◀ *Before it has dried, rub off the liming wax using clear wax and a soft cloth.*

◀◀ *Coloured waxes, applied with a cloth (or strong tissue), can change the colour of wood.*

◀ *Apply gold wax with an old toothbrush (or your finger) and buff off with a soft cloth.*

waxes. These are available in a range of wood colours and the darker colours are particularly useful for darkening down a rather brash dye. The method of application is simply to rub sparingly on with a cloth and then to buff it off. If you have not achieved sufficient density, the process can be repeated.

A gold wax can also be used to change the colour of dyed wood slightly or to heighten a certain part of the moulding. Apply with an old toothbrush, or even your finger if you wish to cover large areas, and use a circular motion when applying to eliminate uneven application.

Buffing with a soft cloth will help to spread the wax and take away any excess. If you want to gild one specific edge of a moulding, it is better to use gold paint which will give you a crisper finish.

COLOURED VARNISHES

You can buy coloured varnishes in a small range of colours which can be applied to bare wood with a paint brush. I find that the best method of application is to give several thin coats to get the colour that you want, as one heavy application tends to run and form pools.

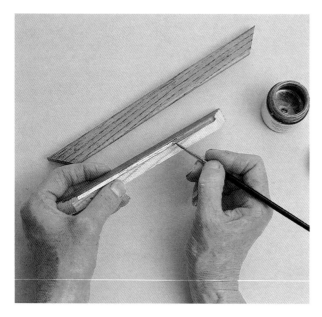

▲ *A gold 'sight-edge' can be created by using gold paint applied with a fine artist's brush.*

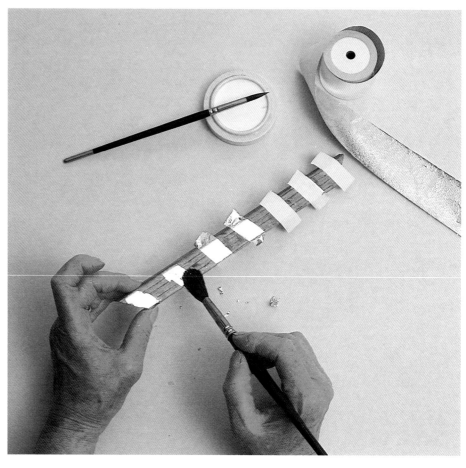

▶ *Metal leaf can be applied to a frame in any pattern you like, once gold size has been 'painted' on to the moulding. After the backing paper has been peeled off, excess leaf can be removed with a brush.*

USING PAINT

The small pots of paint sold for model making are ideal for decorating frames – they are sold with either matt or gloss finishes. Apply with a paint brush and leave plenty of time for each coat to dry. When you apply the paint to bare wood you will probably find that you need three coats to give a really good finish.

The new water-based artists' paints are also ideal. The colours can be mixed, but are quick to dry and the brushes can be washed out in water. Because this paint does not soak into the wood like water-based wood dyes, it produces a different, rather more opaque effect. A good combination can be achieved on a moulding with a sculptured profile by carefully applying water-based dye to one part of the moulding, allowing it to dry, then mixing artists' paint to exactly the same colour and painting it on the rest of the moulding. This pro-

duces an interesting gradation of colour. I find this paint is also the best for sponging on to moulding and for stencilling no-frame frames on to borders. I use the paint without dilution to produce a rather crusty effect, but I mix the colours to tone with areas in the picture.

Gold paints can be used to give a sight-edge or a thin gold line. All gold paint requires stirring very carefully and should be applied with a fine artist's brush which should be thoroughly cleaned afterwards.

APPLYING METAL LEAF

First paint the gold size on to the frame in the desired pattern, allow the size to become tacky, carefully cut off small pieces of the metal leaf together with its backing paper and apply to the sized areas. It will stick instantly, the backing paper can be peeled off and any excess leaf can be brushed away with a soft mop brush.

Decorating mounts

There is a wonderful choice of ways in which you can decorate a mount, all of which are carried out after the aperture has been cut in the finished size.

LINING RECTANGULAR MOUNTS

The simplest form of mount decoration is lining and, with normal rectangular and square mounts, starts with the use of a corner gauge.

Take the 'practice' mount that you cut earlier, tuck the gauge into the cut corner of the aperture and mark off the same two or three measurements on each corner. These, when joined up, will give lines to lead the eye into the picture. This is ample for a mount with borders of 3cm (1¼in). If you want to draw more lines (or to have a washline – see page 36), the borders would have to be cut wider to accommodate them.

With a bevelled-edge ruler turned on its face to avoid blotting, carefully join the marks to form lines. Try using fibre-tipped pens in subtle colours, gold pens and also a ruling pen filled with paint for different effects.

Now, with the ruling pen, try mixing colours, aiming for a range that complement a picture. There is nothing quite as nice as a line drawn with a ruling pen, for not only can you choose your own colours, but you can alter the width of the line as well. I use either watercolour or diluted artists' colours in lining pens: both are equally good. If you want a gold line, mix gold acrylic paint with a little water and keep it in a small screw-topped jar; it should last for several weeks.

APPLIED DECORATIONS

The next thing to try is using your corner gauge to mark out for applied self-adhesive strip decoration. Tuck the gauge into the corners of the aperture and mark points that are well away from the cut edge. Hold the strip roughly along the sides of the mount and tear off four pieces that will be long enough to cross at the corners. Remove the backing paper and gently line the strip up to the marks taking care that it is not pressed down until it is correctly positioned. Then press the centre of each strip lightly to hold it in place.

▼ *Lines can be drawn with fibre-tipped pens, gold pens or a ruling pen, used against a ruler held with its bevel edge facing downwards.*

▲ *The starting point for most mount decoration is to use a corner gauge, tucked into the corner of the aperture, to mark the position of the decoration across the corners.*

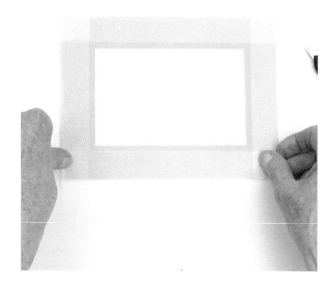

◀ *To apply self-adhesive strip decoration, first use a corner gauge to mark its position and then carefully lay the strips between the marks.*

▶ *When just one area of the mount is to be decorated, apply lengths of wide 'magic' finger-lift tape around the mount, after first marking it out with a corner gauge.*

▼ *Sponging a (masked) mount is an easy method of decoration and can be done with any number of colours to match the picture.*

Using a very sharp scalpel or craft knife and a small straight-edge, the corners can now be mitred. Cut carefully on the same line through the top layer and the lower layer, removing the excess. The two cut edges should fit neatly together forming a perfect mitre.

The corner gauge is also used to mark mounts before applying instant corner motifs and flourishes. These need to be used with discretion but can be very effective. They can be used on their own or combined with lines.

MASKING MOUNTS

For techniques such as sponging or spraying, you will need to make a mask. This is done by covering parts of the mount with finger-lift magic tape leaving an area exposed for decoration.

With your 'practice' mount, tuck the corner gauge into the corners of the aperture and mark off two measurements about 1.5cm (or ½in) apart. Between these marks is the area that will be decorated. Tape the outer line first using your marks as the guide and crossing the tape at the corners. More care is needed at the corners when taping the inner line – these can either be mitred or crossed providing that no tape protrudes on to the area between the two tape lines.

SPONGING

This is one of the easiest forms of mount decoration. First mask the mount then cut pieces from a synthetic sponge keeping a separate piece for every colour that you want to use. Using slightly diluted artists' paint, mix three colours – preferably one dark, one medium and one pale – that link with the picture and choose the darkest of the three to start with. Dip the sponge into the paint and get rid of any excess on a piece of kitchen roll. Pat the sponge on to the exposed area of the mount at intervals all round keeping the application even.

Allow a short while for this to dry and then repeat the process with the medium colour, filling in any gaps that may have been left. Finally, and very delicately, apply the pale colour taking care that it does not obscure the other two colours. When all the paint is thoroughly dry remove the tapes and you should have a mottled border with clean straight edges. This can be further enhanced with gold lines.

SPRAYING

Mask the mount as before and mix watercolours that will link with the picture or use a child's airbrush, selecting the coloured felt-tip pens that will suit. Spray one colour sparingly on to the exposed area and immediately spray on another. You will find that this has the effect of colour mixing so that blue and yellow will look green, and blue and red will look purple. A third colour can be used to enhance the effect, either all round or in selected areas.

Try masking with a scrap piece of mountboard and changing the colours as you go to produce a candy-stripe effect, or mask with a combination of other shapes and tape to produce interesting patterns.

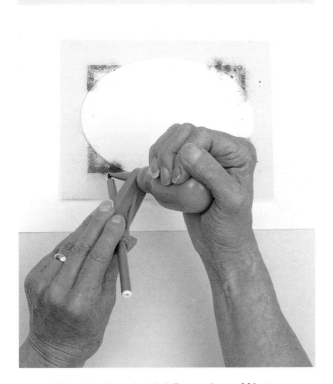

▲ *A child's airbrush, used with different colours of felt-tip pen, provides a delicate but effective method of mount decoration.*

▲ *Using an oval mask with a child's airbrush (as in the photograph left) produces this interesting decorative effect.*

DECORATING WITH CUT SHAPES OR BUDS

The exposed area of a masked mount can be decorated with cut shapes of board dipped into paint, cotton buds dipped into paint or any other ingenious idea that you may have for transferring paint on to the surface. An effective method that I use frequently is to dip the edge of a thick piece of cardboard into the paint, putting the edge down on to the exposed area and dragging it slightly so that it makes an attractive graded mark. A second colour can be added between the first marks if required. I have used both card and buds in my *Child's painting* project on page 60.

WASHLINING

This traditional form of mount decoration for water-colours is a much sought-after skill and the mount must be cut with much wider borders than usual, 9 to 10cm (3½ to 4in), to accommodate it. The marks for the lines are made using the corner gauge, as for normal lining, but the design can vary.

A good combination for washlining is to make marks at 0.5cm, 1cm, 3cm and 5cm (³⁄₁₆in, ³⁄₈in, 1¼in and 2in). The inside mark at 0.5cm is called the *sight line*, the two middle marks at 1cm and 3cm will be either side of the *wash* and the outer mark at 5cm is called the *lead line*. The whole point of a washline is that it leads the eye comfortably into the watercolour and tones and harmonises with it, so the colours must be picked out of the picture and each watercolour should be given its own washline. This makes the whole thing very special.

Mix two washes of paint in separate containers, choosing one dark colour and one light colour to tone with the painting. Adjust the ruling pen to a medium line and fill it with the darker of the two washes. Turn a ruler face down to avoid blotting and position it on the outside of the mount lined up on the inner (sight line)

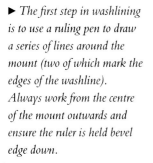

► *The first step in washlining is to use a ruling pen to draw a series of lines around the mount (two of which mark the edges of the washline). Always work from the centre of the mount outwards and ensure the ruler is held bevel edge down.*

marks. Carefully rule the first line, turn the mount, reposition the ruler, refill the pen and rule the next line. Provided the ruler is kept on the outside of the mount, all four inner sight lines can be ruled like this without waiting for the paint to dry on the previous one as there will be no chance of smudging.

Clean out the pen, adjust to widen the line and refill using the paler of the two washes. Position the ruler on the next set of marks (the inside of the washline) and rule the next line around the mount turning it and refilling the pen each time. Move the ruler to the next set of marks and repeat the process with the same colour paint. Lastly, clean out the pen again, adjust it back to a medium line, fill it with the darker colour and draw the outer set of lines for the lead line.

Although this seems like a lengthy process there can be no short cuts without either waiting for each line to dry, or smudging the previous line, but I find that a rhythm develops which makes it quite pleasant to do.

An option is to put an additional fine gold line on the outside of the outer (lead) line and close to it, which is done with the mix of gold acrylic paint and water. This gives the washline a little sparkle without making it look vulgar. Allow all the lines to become completely dry before progressing to the wash.

Take a little of the paler colour and dilute it in a third dish to make the wash, using a lot of water until it is very faint. With a 12mm (½in) flat sable artists brush carefully paint plain clean water between the two wash line markers around the mount without stopping. Immediately fill the brush with the pale wash and paint that around the mount taking care to keep within your ruled lines. The fact that water has been painted on first will help the wash disperse and spread, but there is no worry about the lines smudging providing they were completely dry before you started.

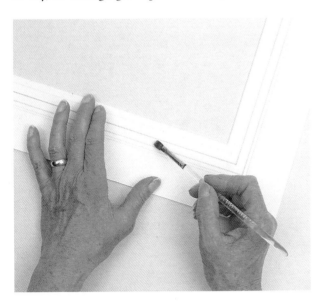

▲ *After mixing up the wash colour you need (so that it is ready), 'paint' the area for the washline between the lines with plain clean water, working round the mount without stopping.*

▶ *Immediately after the clean water has been applied, use the same brush to apply the pale wash, taking care to stay within the ruled lines.*

Projects

The basic framing techniques and the basic decoration techniques now have to be combined to suit the item to be framed. This is enormous fun and the ideas are endless. The inspiration can start with the design and finish of an old frame, with the picture itself or even with the colour of a piece of mountboard.

Sepia photograph of great-grandma

A friend recently brought me an old photograph of her great grandmother to frame. It is a lovely sepia colour and I was able to find an old oak frame to cut down for it. I also had fun experimenting with some new instant mount decorations.

You will need

Preparation
- Old oak frame to be cut down
- Pre-cut mount in pale peach with an oval aperture
- Basic framing kit

Decoration
- Spirit wood dye in medium oak
- Sheet of adhesive mount decorations in sepia

Assembly
- Basic assembly kit

PREPARATION

When you are cutting down a old frame, try to choose one that is much larger than you need because then it does not matter if you damage the corners when you take it apart. This can happen as you try to remove the excessively long nails that were always used on old frames: if these nails are not removed and the saw hits one, it blunts the blade very quickly. If the frame has still got its glass and backing board, you can re-use these, cutting them down to size.

When a frame is being cut down, it is far better to make new cuts on all the corners, even if some of them do not look too bad. New cuts will ensure that the frame will fit together perfectly so the first task is to cut the long sides to 25cm (or 10in) plus ease and the short sides to 20cm (or 8in) plus ease and join them as normal.

While I was pinning my frame I noticed that there were one or two rough pieces at the corners, so I disguised these with a little medium oak spirit dye spread over the frame with a wad of cotton wool.

An oval aperture in the mount not only looks attractive but is very appropriate for this period of photograph. You may be able to buy a ready-made mount with an oval already cut in it; if not, ask your local picture framer to cut an oval in pale peach mountboard with the border at the bottom wider than at the top and sides to accommodate the design.

DECORATION

You will not want to overdo the decoration on this mount, so choose two designs from the sheet that make a pair. As mount decorations like these are very conveniently printed on clear squared plastic it is easy to experiment with where to place each design. When you have finally decided on the positions, measure and make guide marks and then transfer the designs on to the board by scribbling on the surface of the plastic with a pencil or ballpoint pen.

ASSEMBLY

Lay the photograph face up on the table and use two pieces of masking tape across the corners to fasten the mount in place as described on page 27. You can then turn the photograph and mount over and apply additional pieces of masking tape to make it really secure.

1 If there are any rough or damaged corners of the frame once you have cut it down and re-assembled it, disguise these with wood spirit dye applied with cotton wool.

The glass and backing board need to be cut down to the same measurement as the mount. If you are cutting down old glass, take care that you cut the piece of glass from the centre, away from the dirty edges. This may seem a little wasteful but the offcuts can rarely be used, and the edges are usually almost impossible to clean.

The frame is assembled in the normal way and a normal strength cord used. Alternatively, if the photograph and frame are fairly small and light, a small decorative hanger could be pinned on the top at the back or, for standing on a shelf or cupboard, a stand-up or 'strut' back can be fitted.

2 *Decide where you want to put your applied decorations and then make a light pencil mark on the mount.*

3 *Position the sheet of decorations over your marks and transfer the design on to the mount by rubbing the back of the sheet with a pencil or a ball-point pen.*

4 *Once all the decoration has been applied to the mount, it can be secured to the photograph and assembled into the frame in the normal way.*

Shell mirror

I found this collection of shells at a car boot sale and decided that they would make a good decoration for a bathroom mirror. The shells are large so I needed to use a moulding with a wide flat profile so that I could stick the arrangements safely to it.

You will need

Preparation
- Plain moulding
- Clear wax
- Basic framing kit

Decoration
- Wood adhesive
- Shells of different sizes
- Self-hardening modelling clay

Assembly
- 3mm mirror glass cut to fit frame
- Hardboard to fit frame
- Basic assembly kit

PREPARATION

First cut the moulding into four pieces with an inside measurement of 23cm (9in), rub down with wire wool and wax each piece with clear wax, applied with a soft cloth, before joining them to make the frame.

DECORATION

With the frame flat on a table, you can start to arrange the shells on it. It's best to place the largest shells in the centre and arrange the others in clusters around them to produce a symmetrical pattern. Where the shells have interesting mother of pearl on the insides, reverse them so that this will show.

Once you are happy with the arrangement, gently remove the shells from each side at a time, so that you can replace them in exactly the same order with generous helpings of wood adhesive and then allow everything to dry overnight.

The next day you hope to find that everything is firm and dry. But, because of the lovely curving shapes of the shells, you may find some big gaps between them and the frame which need to be filled with the clay. Each gaping hole should be filled, smoothed off with a cotton bud dipped into water, and allowed to dry for two days. It is easy to tell when the clay is dry because it turns from a rather grey colour to white. Check the effect carefully and sand off any remaining rough edges with fine sandpaper.

ASSEMBLY

When the clay is completely dry, put the frame face down on a soft cushion to protect the shells and place the piece of mirror into it. This should always be a snug

1 After cutting the moulding to size, rub it down to a smooth finish with fine-grade wire wool.

2 Apply clear wax to the moulding with a cloth or kitchen tissue once the surface is smooth.

fit, as should the hardboard which is placed on top. Now fasten the 'sandwich' securely as normal taking care not to press down too hard, which could damage the shells.

Finally, with the mirror still face down on the cushion, tape the back and fit screw eyes plus a medium thickness picture cord, used double thickness because of the weight of the mirror.

3 *Take some time arranging the shells to produce a symmetrical pattern with the biggest shells in the centre of each arrangement. Reverse any mother-of-pearl shells.*

4 *The individual shells are held in place with wood adhesive once you are happy with the arrangement and, when the adhesive has dried, any gaps are filled with clay.*

Kitchen memo board

My love affair with blue and white pottery started years ago and I use it all the time, hanging my chipped plates on the kitchen walls. But inevitably there are breakages, which I hate to throw away. I needed a kitchen memo board, so decided to smash my breakages into even smaller pieces and use them as a mosaic. I have even been able to add blue and white shards that I dug up in the garden. It is interesting to think that I am not the first person in this old house that liked blue and white pottery.

You will need

Preparation
• Old frame
• Softboard to fit it
• White acrylic paint
• White gloss paint
• Fine sandpaper
• 000 wire wool

Decoration
• Selection of broken pottery
• Heavy hammer
• Heavy-duty clear polythene bag
• Ceramic tile adhesive/grout
• Clear varnish
• Blue gloss paint

Assembly
• Basic assembly kit

PREPARATION

An old frame is often very dirty (this one was found in a box of junk at an auction), so the first job is usually to clean it thoroughly, then lightly sand it and finally give it a good rub with wire wool to remove any grease. When the frame is ready, undercoat it with acrylic paint and then paint two coats of gloss on the back, the top of the rebate and the sight-edge. Also apply two coats of white acrylic paint to the smooth side of the softboard allowing the first coat to dry before applying the second.

1 The best way to break up china or pottery is to put it into a polythene bag and then hit them with a hammer, holding the neck of the bag tightly.

DECORATION

You will need to wash the pieces of broken pottery and sort them into types and colours – I found that there were many different blues. Then put all the pieces of each type into a polythene bag and, holding the neck tightly to prevent pieces flying about, smash them into tiny pieces with the hammer. The resulting collection of shards can then be tipped on to a sheet of paper and sorted. Discard boring plain white pieces and also pieces that are too curved or shaped on the back to lie down properly, but you might like to keep pieces that have the makers name in blue because they are fun to include. Soon you will be surrounded by piles of broken pottery in different blues on separate sheets of paper.

There is usually an applicator included in a pot of ceramic tile adhesive but it is rather clumsy and large for this purpose, so cut a strip off it to make a more delicate tool. You also need a narrow-bladed tool (I used a palette knife) to help in positioning the shards.

Apply a generous amount of adhesive to the top of the frame, covering about 10cm (4in), and smooth it out with the applicator trying to line it up at the sides. Select from the piles of shards and start to nestle each piece into the adhesive taking care that they are level and also that no two pieces from the same plate are side by side. When the first section is complete, tidy up the edges with a cotton bud dipped in water, removing any over-hanging adhesive and smooth it off.

As tile adhesive/grout starts to dry out quite quickly forming a hard crust, you must not leave a section half completed, so this decoration means progressing round the frame in small steps. When one section is finished, a new one can be started immediately, the next day or even the next week, so there is no need to labour over this rather long job.

The next stage is to grout between the pieces of pottery where necessary. Delicately add more tile adhesive/grout between the pieces with a cotton bud, clean

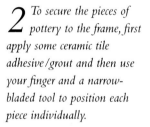

2 To secure the pieces of pottery to the frame, first apply some ceramic tile adhesive/grout and then use your finger and a narrow-bladed tool to position each piece individually.

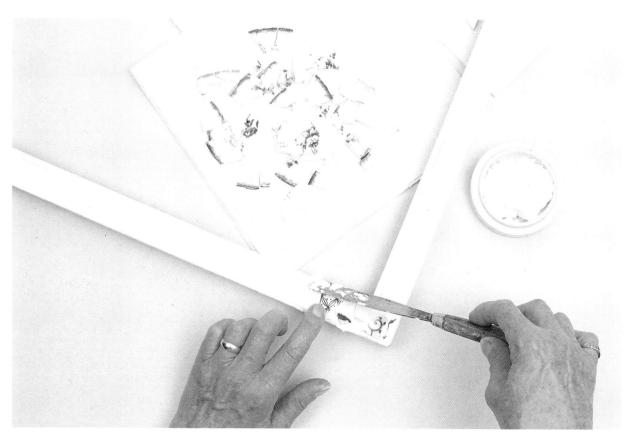

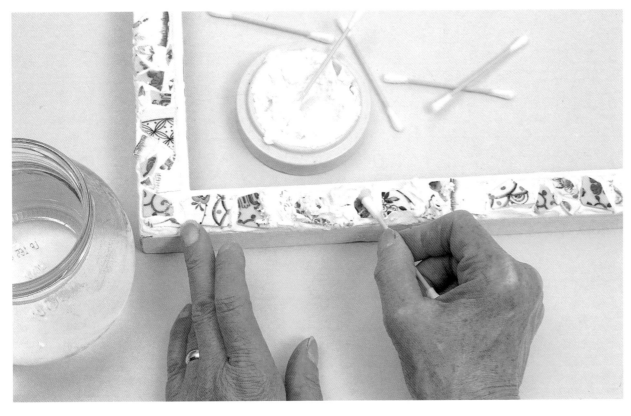

3 Once all the pieces of pottery have been attached, add more adhesive/grout to fill the gaps between the pieces and polish the surface of each piece with a cotton bud.

4 To give the softboard a border, draw faint pencil lines in from the edge and paint between them with a fine brush and the colour of your choice.

up immediately with another bud dipped in water, and finish off by polishing each shard with a dry bud. Also fill any gaps in the adhesive on the edges at this stage.

The decoration must be left to dry completely before the final inspection when any overhangs can be easily sanded off.

If you want a border on the softboard, finger-lift tape is no good as a mask because the board is so absorbent that the paint seeps underneath, so it is best to paint it by hand. Measure 4cm (1½in) in from all four edges of the softboard, then a further 0.5cm (³⁄₁₆in) all round for the inner edge and rule faint pencil lines. With the blue gloss paint and a fine artist's brush carefully paint between these lines.

ASSEMBLY

Lay the frame face down on a soft cloth to protect the surface, place the softboard in it and assemble in the normal way, using large screw eyes and double-thickness nylon cord as the frame will be heavy.

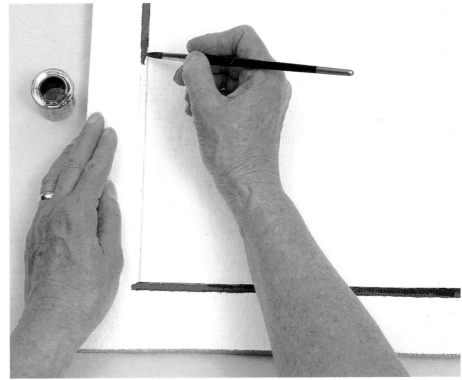

P r i n t   o f   O l d   M a s t e r

This beautiful reproduction of Giotto's St Francis was on a calendar and I admired the composition and rich colours. I deliberately picked out an ivory colour for the double mount to accentuate the richness and then used an applied marbled decoration. To complete the look, I searched for a moulding that had a classic but 'distressed' finish in old gold.

You will need

Preparation
- Print
- Length of old gold moulding 4cm (1½in) wide
- Two pieces of mount board in ivory
- Basic framing kit
- Basic mount cutting kit

Decoration
- Two rolls of marbled mount decoration in brown 1.5cm and 0.5cm (or ⅝in and ¼in) wide
- Double-sided tape
- Basic mount decoration kit

Assembly
- Glass
- Hardboard
- Basic assembly kit

PREPARATION

Cut two pieces of moulding 56cm (22in) plus ease and two pieces 46.5cm (18¼in) plus ease and make the frame as normal. While the adhesive is setting, you can cut the two ivory mounts to the same overall size, but one with equal borders of 7cm (2¾in) and the other with equal borders of 9cm (3½in).

DECORATION

Using a corner gauge set into the corners of the apertures, mark both boards at 0.5cm (or ¼in). Then tear off four pieces of the narrower marbled decoration and apply them to the mount with the wider borders and, similarly apply four lengths of the wider marbled mount decoration to the mount with the narrower borders, mitring both decorative strips neatly at the corners and removing the excess as described on page 34.

Fasten the double mount together as described on page 27. Be very careful to align the two mounts when you do this as double-sided tape is extremely sticky and it is very difficult to separate two mounts that have been incorrectly stuck together.

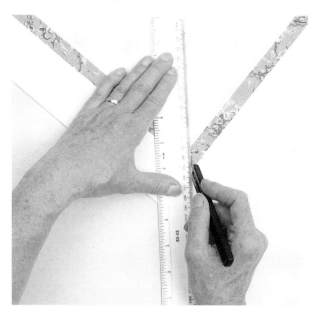

1 Once the position of the marbled decoration has been marked out on the mounts, it can be applied, using tiny slips of paper at the corners to stop the ends sticking down.

2 Each corner should be mitred with a scalpel, cutting through both strips at the same time, and the excess (and the paper slips) removed.

ASSEMBLY

Place the print face up on the table and slip two pieces of masking tape under it projecting out top and bottom, then lower the double mount on to the print pressing down when it is in the correct position. Place the frame face down on a table, clean the glass and put it into the frame immediately followed by the double mounts and finally the backing board. Fasten securely and tape the back. As this picture is not very heavy, standard screw eyes and medium-weight cord can be used.

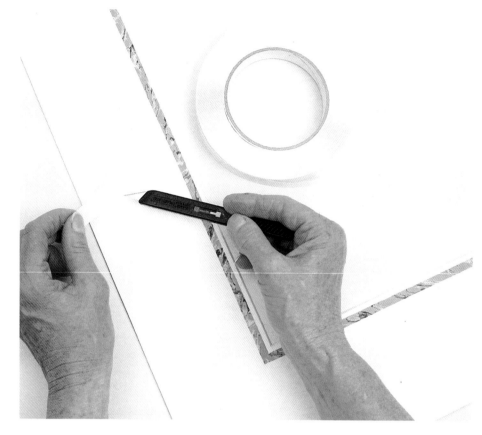

3 The double mount is held together with double-sided adhesive tape. Stick this down firmly to the lower mount before removing the backing tape.

4 Take great care when positioning the upper mount on top of the lower one – the adhesive tape is very strong and mistakes are almost impossible to correct.

Print-room effect

I visited a splendid print room in a large country house recently and have been very influenced by it. But instead of having a whole room covered with prints, which was the eighteenth century fashion, I decided to decorate just a small wall area in the same way.

First, I selected one or two fashion prints from my own collection that I particularly liked. Then I hunted through my books for a good selection of engravings of frames and borders. I took the prints, frames and borders to be photocopied, making sure that the frames were enlarged so that they fitted the fashion prints exactly.

You will need

Preparation
- One or two fashion prints (or photocopies)
- Prints of borders and frames (or photocopies)
- Plain white paper
- Glass sheets
- Cat litter tray
- Cold tea
- Weights

Decoration and assembly
- Wallpaper paste
- Blu-tack
- Artists' matt varnish

PREPARATION

The only trouble with normal photocopying paper is that it is so very white and somehow the alternative cream paper was also not the colour that I wanted, so I decided to stain everything myself. To do this, make up a weak tea mixture, pour it into a large shallow dish, (a cat litter tray is an ideal shape) put a piece of glass into the tray and lay a print in the liquid for a few minutes until it is ivory coloured. Then lift out the glass with the print on it and drain off the excess liquid.

The prints will dry quite happily on the pieces of glass, but if they become a little cockled, put them between plain white paper under a board with some weights on top for a day or two.

1 A mixture of weak cold tea in a large shallow dish is an ideal way of staining prints to a uniform ivory colour. The print is laid on a sheet of glass and lifted out after a few minutes. Leave on the glass to dry.

DECORATION

Cut out the frames and the prints, lay them on a flat surface and move them around until you are happy with the overall arrangement.

Mark the wall lightly with a pencil to give an indication of the position of each piece, fasten them temporarily to the wall with Blu-tack and stand back to check the proportions and overall effect.

ASSEMBLY

When you are satisfied you have got the positions right, mix up some wallpaper paste following the instructions for standard wallpaper, coat the back of each print and place it in its position on the wall, using a soft clean cloth to smooth it flat without rubbing too hard. Then start to build up the pattern of 'frames' and borders, pasting and placing one piece at a time.

When the whole area is completely dry, protect the entire design with two coats of artists' matt varnish.

2 Once dry after staining, cut out the prints and the photocopied 'frames' and arrange them roughly on a flat surface.

3 On your flat surface, try different combinations of print, 'frame' and decorative border moving them around until you have achieved the effect you want.

4 Having tried out various positions and arrangements of the pictures, stick the prints, frames and decorative borders to the wall using wallpaper paste and protect with varnish.

Miniature beaded frames

I wanted to make some photograph frames that I could stand in a group together and maybe add to in the future. I like the decoration on jewellery and enamelware that was popular in the 1930's, so thought that I would try to simulate it using beads instead of precious stones.

You will need

Preparation
- Scrap plywood
- Sandpaper
- Fine-grade (000) wire wool
- Saws for wood

Decoration
- Small threaded dress beads in various colours
- Artists' paint in colours to tone
- Liquid PVA adhesive
- Artists' clear varnish

Assembly
- Small pieces of acetate film
- Small stand-up back for each frame
- Hardboard
- Craft knife and straight-edge
- Basic assembly kit

PREPARATION

The size of the frames will obviously depend on the photographs you are using and the cut-out can be any shape you want – square, rectangular, round or oval. For these photographs, I decided to make one rectangular frame 8.5 × 10.5cm (or 3¼ × 4in) with a cut-out of 3.5 × 5cm (or 1½ by 2in) and a second oval frame with the same overall dimensions, but with an oval aperture – see the shapes below.

If you have the correct saws, you may be able to make your own cut-outs, but this is something you might want to leave (as I did) to a carpenter friend.

Cutting plywood is not difficult once you have marked out the shape – you can cut it to size with a tenon saw and cut the aperture with a padsaw (drilling one or more holes to start the saw off). If you own (or can borrow) an electric jigsaw, it will make the cutting that much faster.

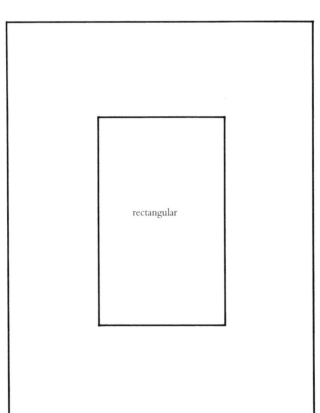

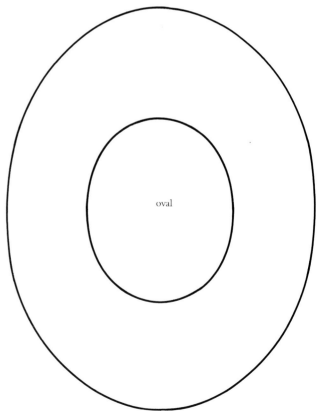

The shapes for the frames

1 With the frames cut to size from plywood, and sanded and rubbed with wire wool until smooth, start by marking out each frame into different areas with lines running in different directions.

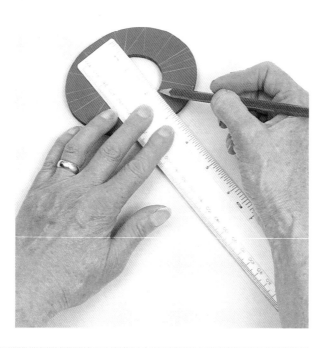

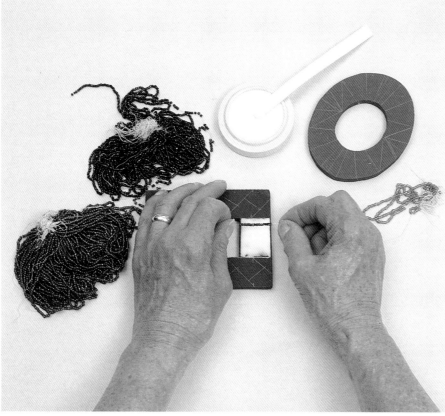

DECORATION

Once the frames have been cut to size, sand each one carefully and then rub with wire wool until they are silky smooth. Work out what colour scheme you are going to use – I used two coats of paynes grey on the rectangular frame and two coats of terracotta on the oval frame.

When the paint is dry, mark out the shapes you want with pencil on the frames to act as a guide while sticking on the beads. To reflect the most light and to make the beads sparkle, they should be laid in different directions – so divide the area up as much as possible.

Coat one small area with PVA adhesive and then, very carefully, break the loop of thread on one line of beads. Holding both ends of the thread, lay the line of beads into the adhesive and hold it there for a few seconds. Once the beads have settled into the adhesive, you can gently withdraw the thread.

Repeat this process with the next line and continue until the whole glued area has been filled with beads. Then move on to the next area of the same colour and repeat the process. When you want to divide two colours with a different line, use the same method, but with greater care on the longer strings of beads.

When the whole frame is filled with beads, allow it to dry and set overnight and then coat the surface liberally with artist's clear varnish in order to secure all the beads from the top. This will take a further two hours to dry.

ASSEMBLY

Using a craft knife and a small straight-edge, cut three short hardboard strips 8mm (or ¼in) wide and 6 strips 4mm (or ⅛in) wide for each frame. Cut the strips 5cm (2in) long and stick the narrower strips together in pairs. When the adhesive has set, stick each pair to the wider strip, so that one of the long edges lines up to make a L-shaped channel.

2 Coat one area with PVA adhesive, then break one end of the thread and lay a line of beads into the adhesive before withdrawing the thread.

Now cut down a stand-up back so that it will cover the aperture in the frame and also trim the support leg making sure that the frame will stand up, leaning slightly backwards as it should. Tape the stand-up back temporarily into position and place the hardboard channels on either side and below it. When it is all correct, glue the channels in place and leave to set.

Glass would make these frames too heavy, so it would be better to use acetate film to protect the photographs: simply cut a small rectangle of film which can be slid into place with the photograph into the channels together with the stand-up back.

3 *Each glued area is filled with beads running in the same direction – but the direction is altered for the adjacent area to reflect light and to make the beads sparkle.*

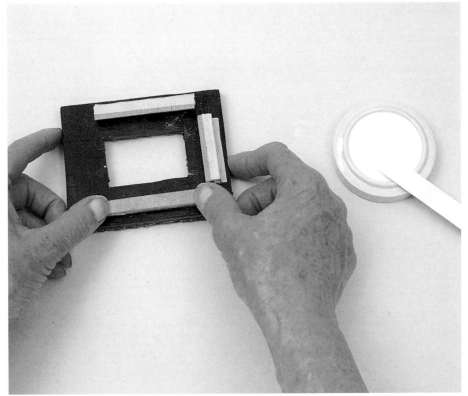

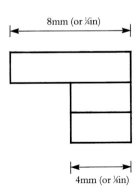

The three hardboard strips are glued together as shown to form the L-shaped channels.

4 *To provide support for the photograph and also for the stand-up back, the L-shaped hardboard channels are glued to the back of the frame.*

Child's painting

Children's or grandchildren's paintings are such fun to display, but I feel that framing them with the conventional mount and frame is a little too formal. On the other hand, if they are just taped on the wall they can get torn. This project, using a softboard backing and a painted mount, is an answer to both problems, creating a bright, lively yet inexpensive presentation that will make everyone proud.

You will need

Preparation
- Child's painting
- Softboard 10cm (or 4in) larger all round than the painting
- Deep blue mountboard the same size as the softboard
- Wood sealer
- Basic mount cutting kit

Decoration
- Artists' paints in colours to suit the painting
- Basic mount decoration kit

Assembly
- Masking tape
- Liquid PVA adhesive
- Wooden board and weights

PREPARATION

The edges of softboard are often a little rough and crumbly, so start by sanding them gently and apply two coats of wood sealer, extending it slightly over the edges on to the front and back of the softboard. The first coat will be sucked in immediately, but a second coat should be sufficient to give a base for paint.

When the sealer is dry, turn the softboard face down, and on the rough reverse side of the board mark a point 7.5cm (3in) down from the top and in the centre. To make the hanger hole, draw a short line of about 2cm (¾in) at this point as a guide and then two more lines of the same length to form an upside-down triangle.

Use a scalpel and a small straight-edge as a guide to cut around the triangle and remove enough of the softboard to enable a wall-mounted nail or picture hook to lodge inside it.

On the mountboard, measure and mark a border 10cm (or 4in) wide all round and use a hand-held mount cutter to cut the aperture.

DECORATION

Using magic lift-off tape, mask 2cm (¾in) away from the aperture all round and cut a small piece of sponge into a semi-circular shape to link with the shapes on the painting. Using a suitable colour of paint (I chose orange), sponge the mountboard all around the aperture.

When the paint is dry, remove the tape and use more tape to leave a 0.5cm (or ¼in) gap into which you can paint a solid line of the same colour.

Then mask again, leaving a 2.5cm (1in) gap and sponge all round with the paint colour again, leaving a gap of the mountboard between the two sponged areas and on the other side of the tape, paint a solid line of a different colour (in this case, olive green).

When all this paint has dried, complete the decoration by painting some spots within the sponging in a third colour (I used scarlet) and add a broken line against it in the first colour (orange), using the edge of a piece of card to apply the paint.

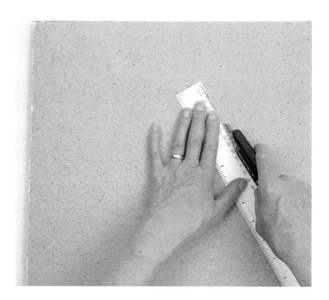

1 To enable the painting to be hung on a wall, a triangular recess is made in the back with the point of the triangle at the top. Cut out the triangular shape with a scalpel, cutting halfway through the board before gouging out the waste.

Finally remove the tapes and finish off by painting some random olive-green patterns in the gap left by the masking tape.

ASSEMBLY

Fasten the painting firmly to the mount with masking tape, making sure that it is flat and secure. Because of the absorbency of the softboard, coat the front of it with liquid PVA adhesive fairly generously and also spread a thin skim to the back of the mountboard but not the picture. Stick the two boards together, taking care to position the mountboard exactly on to the softboard, wipe away any excess adhesive from the edges, place a wooden board and weights on top and leave it to dry.

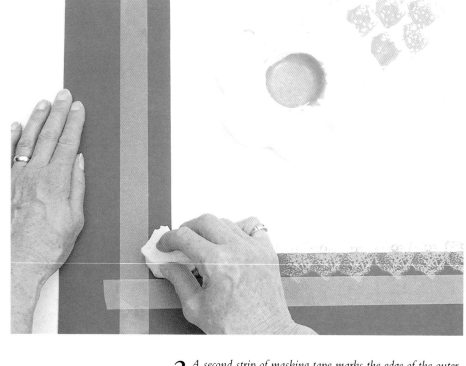

2 Mask off an area of the mountboard around the aperture with magic lift-off tape and sponge all round.

3 A second strip of masking tape marks the edge of the outer sponged area and provides an edge along which the solid line is painted in a different colour.

4 A attractive effect can be created by adding coloured spots within the sponging and then using the edge of a piece of card to apply more paint of the first colour outside the line.

Oil painting on board

An oil painting is usually surrounded with a conventional wide gold frame. But I wanted to give this contemporary oil-on-board a different treatment, while still leading the eye into the painting. By framing the board in a narrow moulding and then raising it from the dark background, the painting is made to look more three-dimensional and seems to acquire depth.

You will need

Preparation
- Oil painting on board
- Plain moulding in a deep 'hockey stick' profile
- Blockboard or thick plywood 5.5cm (or 2⅛in) larger all round than the painting
- Basic framing kit

Decoration
- Basic frame decoration kit

Assembly
- Wood adhesive
- Basic assembly kit

PREPARATION

Cut the frame mouldings to the size of the oil-on-board – in this case a standard 56 × 40cm (22 × 16in) size – plus ease. The blockboard or plywood should be cut 11cm (or 4¼in) larger – a timber supplier will do this for you if you do not have the saws or the confidence to do it accurately yourself.

DECORATION

Colour the four pieces of moulding with two wood dyes, applying the second before the first one has dried. Pick one of the colours in the painting to dye the frame; for this picture, I found using lavender and antique pine dyes toned with the background and matched the shadows on the man's face.

Then make up a thick mix of colour for the backing board which tones with another part of the painting – in this case, the deep greeny purple in the pullover. This mix is applied in two coats over the edges of the board and 7.5cm (3in) on to the surface all round.

ASSEMBLY

Make up the frame as normal, giving it two coats of clear wax polish to create a sheen and to seal the surface, and fasten the oil painting into the frame.

Mark the backing board carefully 5cm (2in) in from the edges and make small unobtrusive marks on each edge as guides. Apply wood adhesive fairly generously to the back face of the moulding and then lower it gently and carefully into position using the guide marks. Leave the whole thing for twenty-four hours to make

sure that it is perfectly dry before trying to pick it up.

Position screw eyes 7.5cm (3in) down from the top and use a double thickness of medium cord to take the weight of the assembled frame.

1 Once the four lengths of moulding have been cut to size, colour them using cotton wool to apply a dye (or a combination of dyes) to match a colour in the oil painting.

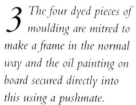

2 *Mix up a second stronger colour, again matching it to the painting, and apply it with a sponge to the edges and outer surface of the board.*

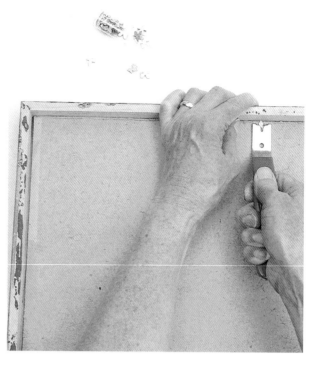

3 *The four dyed pieces of moulding are mitred to make a frame in the normal way and the oil painting on board secured directly into this using a pushmate.*

4 *With light guide marks on the backing board, apply wood adhesive to the back of the frame and lower it gently into place. Leave for twenty-four hours before trying to pick it up.*

Set of flower prints

Sets of prints are always nice to have, and these four flower prints by Charles Rennie Mackintosh are ideal for creating coordinated mounts and frames. I liked the delicate colours on the flowers, so have used pastel colours and a textured mountboard in a cloud design. In order to make the frames look light, I stained and limed the moulding to tone.

You will need

Preparation
- Set of prints
- Two lengths of plain oak moulding about 3cm (1¼in) wide
- Mountboard in pink cloud
- Glass
- Hardboard
- Basic framing kit
- Basic mount cutting kit

Decoration
- Water-based dye in lavender and rose
- Wire wool 000 grade
- Clear wax
- Artists' paints
- Basic frame decoration kit
- Basic mount decoration kit

Assembly
- Basic assembly kit

PREPARATION

Cut eight pieces of moulding 26cm (or 10¼in) plus ease, and eight pieces 21.5 cm (or 8 ½in) plus ease and cut four pieces of mountboard and four pieces of hardboard exactly 26 × 21.5cm (or 10¼ × 8½in). Then cut the four mounts to the same size with equal borders of 4cm (or 1½in) all round.

DECORATION

Dye the moulding pieces first with a light coat of rose, and then immediately with lavender and leave to dry. Because of the number of pieces, work on just two at a time, then another two and so on, to make sure that the rose dye does not dry and produce a different colour.

Take a pad of wire wool and rub in a generous amount of liming wax on two of the lengths, and then rub it off with a soft cloth dipped into clear wax until the liming wax is left only in the grain and in the grooves of the moulding profile. Repeat with two more lengths and continue until all sixteen lengths have been treated and are the same colour. Then assemble the four frames as normal.

Mask the mounts with two borders of finger-lift tape so that there is an exposed area 0.25cm (or ⅛in) from the aperture and 0.5cm (or ¼in) wide.

Now look at the four prints and mix the artists' paint into two colours to link with the colours on the flowers and leaves – I chose a deep red and a dusty green. Find a sponge with very tiny holes and cut off a small piece. Sponge the stronger colour on first, allowing the card colour to show through and, when it is dry, sponge on the second colour. If you want to create highlights, finish by sponging on a light coating of gold acrylic paint mixed with water.

When all the paint is dry, remove the tapes and rule two gold lines with a gold pen, one on the sight-edge, and one 1cm (or ½in) from the sight-edge.

ASSEMBLY

Fasten the prints to the mounts, clean the glass and assemble the pictures. It is important when you are tackling a set of pictures like this that each one is completed before the next is started so that dust does not fall on to the glass you have already cleaned.

1 It's worth experimenting with different colours of dye, applying them in different orders, both before and after the first one has dried. Here, I am putting on lavender dye before the previously-applied rose dye has dried.

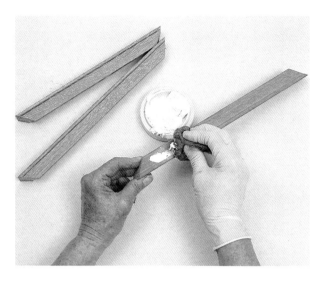

2 Liming wax is applied to the dyed moulding with wire wool and rubbed off with a cloth dipped in clear wax. On a frame of this size, work on just two lengths at a time.

3 With the mount masked by two strips of finger-lift tape, sponge on the colours you have chosen. Here, I am applying a dusty green on top of deep red, to be followed by a light coating of gold to create highlights.

4 Gold lines always enhance pictures like this. I have chosen to use two – one around the sponged decoration and one along the sight-edge (the bevel of the mountboard aperture).

Underwater fish

It is always fun to use the mount and the frame as an extension of the picture, either by continuing the painting on to the mount or, as I have done here, by using decorations suggested by the picture. I wanted to do something a little different with this 19th century engraving of a fish, so I made a mount and frame that suggested an underwater theme.

You will need

Preparation
- Engraving of a fish
- Plain moulding with a flat profile 4cm (or 1½in) wide
- Mountboard in ivory and green pear
- Basic framing kit
- Basic mount cutting kit

Decoration
- Watercolours in shades of green
- Sheet of paper
- Hand spray bottles
- Sample pot of pale green acrylic paint

Assembly
- Glass
- Hardboard
- Double-sided tape
- Basic assembly kit

PREPARATION

Cut the moulding to 35 and 28cm (or 14 and 11in) plus ease and the mounts to the exact measurements. Give the inner mount in green pear 7.5cm (or 3in) borders and the outer, ivory, mount 7cm (or 2¾in) borders.

DECORATION

Give the four pieces of moulding two coats of pale green acrylic paint and put aside to dry. Then cut a continuous curving shape along a piece of paper to create a mask which you can move easily and then mix three shades of green watercolour to enable you to spray

the mount. Put the three colours into small hand spray bottles. It is important to make sure that enough paint of each colour is mixed so that there is no danger of running out partway through the spraying.

Place the mask diagonally across the ivory mount in the top left-hand corner and spray on the first green colour. Then move the mask about 7cm (2¾in) down, keeping it roughly parallel, and spray again repeating the process until you reach the bottom right-hand corner.

Change to a different colour of green, place the mask in the top left-hand corner again, but a little way away from the first spray and repeat the spraying across the

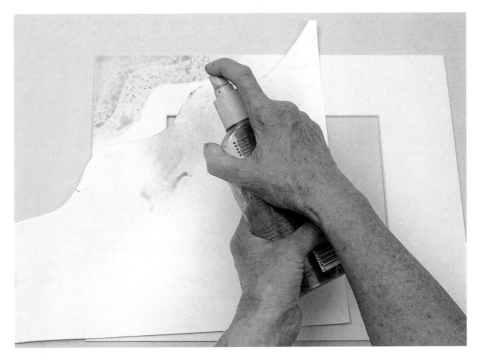

1 Using a curved mask (cut from paper), spray on the first green colour with a simple hand-spray bottle.

mount. To get the curves overlapping and the colours tending to merge (which was exactly the effect that I wanted), take care not to place the mask exactly in line with the previous spray. The third colour can now be sprayed in between the others so that the complete surface of the mount is covered to give an underwater effect. To complete the mount, paint the sight-edge in gold using a very fine sable brush.

Dip your finger into the gold paste and smear it across the surface of the frame in an irregular pattern and then buff it with a soft cloth, making long gentle strokes to allow the pale green to show through.

Finally, using a cotton bud dipped in gold paint, make marks the shape of fish scales in arbitrary groups around the frame. The sight-edge and the outer edge of the frame are left plain.

ASSEMBLY

Fasten the two mounts together using double-sided tape so that 0.5cm (or ¼in) of green pear shows, and then fasten the engraving behind the aperture using masking tape. Assemble the frame in the normal way.

2 After spraying on the second and third green colours (taking care to place the mask in a different position each time), the mount is completed by painting the sight-edge of the mount with gold paint using a fine sable brush.

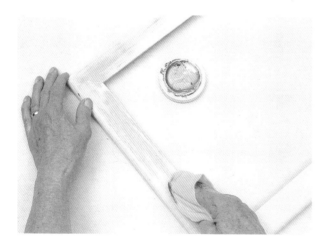

3 The frame has already been painted with pale green acrylic paint, which is enhanced by gold paste smeared across the surface and buffed with a soft cloth.

4 To complete the effect, fish 'scales' are painted on to the frame using a cotton bud dipped in gold paint positioning them in groups round the frame.

Five variations with metal leaf

I wanted to create a group of small frames with a sparkle to hang in a dull corner, so I made these five different little frames, painted or stained them and decorated them with metal leaf or gold wax, so that they could hang together.

You will need

Preparation
- Five small pictures or decorations
- Offcuts of two or three profiles of narrow moulding
- Basic framing kit

Decoration
- Metal leaf
- Gold size
- Basic frame decoration kit

ASSEMBLY
- Five pieces of glass to fit frames if decorative items are not too thick
- Five pieces of hardboard to fit frames
- Basic assembly kit

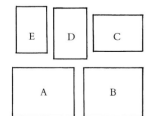

KEY TO PICTURE

PREPARATION

Cut two frames 20 × 15cm (or 8 × 6in) from one moulding and three frames 15 × 10cm (or 6 × 4in) from the other.

The finished frames are shown in the photograph opposite – Frame A (the leaf impressions) is at the bottom left and the letters then go round anti-clockwise to the top left. As I wanted each frame to be decorated differently, I coloured them as follows:

Frame A Dyed with rose and before it was dry again with mahogany.

Frame B Dyed with lavender and then immediately with old pine.

Frame C Painted with red oxide.

Frame D Dyed with lavender, then rose.

Frame E Dyed with apple, then lavender.

When the mouldings are dry, all five frames can be joined in the normal way.

DECORATION

The technique of applying gold leaf to a frame is described and illustrated on page 32.

Frame A Using a cotton bud dipped into the gold size, make random spots around the frame. When the size is tacky (about 20 min), apply small pieces of metal leaf to each spot, pressing them down firmly, remove the paper backing and brush away any excess.

Frame B Using a brush dipped into the gold size, paint diagonal lines around the frame and then apply the metal leaf in the same way.

Frame C Coat the whole frame with gold size, apply metal leaf all round, then use rose dye over the leaf to create an antiqued look.

Frame D Lightly rub the frame with gold wax and burnish with a soft cloth.

Frame E Dip a cotton bud into lavender stain and make random dots around the frame. Repeat with black dots and mask the sides of the frame before painting a black border around the outside back edge of the frame. When the paint is dry, dip a bud into gold size and make more dots. Apply metal leaf as before.

ASSEMBLY

Assemble the frames as normal and pin decorative wreath-top hangers to the centre top of each frame.

1 All the frames are painted or dyed in different ways. Here, I am applying red oxide paint to Frame C which will hang on the right of the top row.

2 On top of the apple and lavender dyes of this frame (Frame E), to hang at the top left, a combination of lavender dye and black paint spots were used, with gold leaf spots as a contrast. Here I am applying the gold-size.

3 For this frame (Frame D), which had been dyed with lavender and then rose and will hang at the top centre, I used gold wax which I burnished with a soft cloth.

4 For this frame (Frame C), which I painted with red oxide in Step 1, gold size was used to coat the whole frame, with metal leaf applied all round and a final light coating of rose dye to give an 'antique' effect.

Greetings card

There are so many greetings cards on sale now that I would like to frame. I was attracted to this one because of the compact composition and the bright colours which I felt would look good if they were to be echoed in the mount decoration.

You will need
Preparation
- Greetings card in bold colours
- Short length of narrow plain moulding
- Mountboard in Pampas
- Basic framing kit
- Basic mount cutting kit

Decoration
- Spirit-based dye in blue
- Child's felt-tip pen airbrush
- Basic mount decoration kit

Assembly
- Hardboard
- Glass
- Basic assembly kit

PREPARATION

Cut the mountboard, backing board and glass to 24 × 20 cm (or 9½ × 7⅞in) and cut the moulding to the same size plus ease. Cut the aperture in the mount to give 4cm (or 1½in) equal borders.

DECORATION

Stain all four pieces of moulding with one coat of blue spirit-based dye and leave to dry.

Mask the mount with finger-lift tape, leaving an exposed area 6mm (or ¼in) away from the sight-edge and 1.5cm (or ⅝in) wide. The felt-tip pen kit that came with the child's airbrush had the colours I needed to link with the picture, but you should experiment for the best effect. I decided on a candy-striped effect using an offcut of mountboard as a very simple mask. To do this, first insert a blue pen into the airbrush and, with the mask lying diagonally across the tapes, spray a small area. Then change the pen to red, move the mask along a little and spray again and, finally, changing the pen to yellow, move the mask by an equal amount and spray a third time. After the yellow stripe, leave a larger gap so that the green of the mountboard shows through and then start the sequence again.

When you reach a corner, turn the mountboard and start down the next side. On the last side, judge the amount of space left by eye to make sure that the sequence will fit in.

The ink dries immediately, so you will be able to remove the tapes and to rule gold lines either side of the band of candy stripe to finish off.

ASSEMBLY

Assemble the frame in the normal way.

1 Cut the moulding to the required size and stain it with a colour to suit one of the main colours in the greetings card chosen.

2 To achieve this 'candy-striped' effect, use at least three colours plus the base colour of the mountboard. Mask the mountboard and spray with the child's airbrush, with the appropriate colour of felt-tip pen inserted, moving the cardboard mask an equal amount each time.

3 At each corner, try to finish with a whole stripe and then turn the mountboard to work along the next side. At the last corner, make sure the sequence is completed.

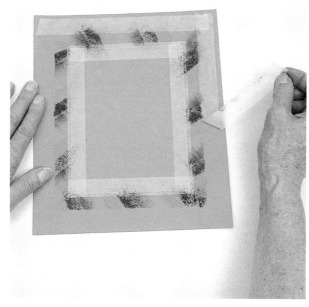

4 As soon as you have finished spraying, remove the lift-off tapes and rule the gold lines.

K*itchen poster*

I wanted to frame this reproduction of an old poster for my kitchen with an 'antiqued' finish and so decided to use a sprayed technique which gives the appearance of an old piece of fabric.

You will need

Preparation
- Old poster
- 9mm plywood
- Wood sealer

Decoration
- Artists' paints in parchment, brilliant orange, cadmium red and magenta
- Hand-spray bottle
- Basic frame decoration kit

Assembly
- Craft knife and straight-edge
- Hardboard
- Wood adhesive

PREPARATION

You will need the plywood to be cut to size with an aperture leaving 7cm (2¾in) borders all round the poster. If you do not feel up to this, a carpenter will be able to do it for you. Sand the cut board thoroughly, particularly on the edges, rub it with fine wire wool and finally coat it all over with wood sealer.

DECORATION

Use a brush to apply two coats of a pale ivory colour – which you can get by mixing parchment and a little brilliant orange – to the plywood frame, rubbing the whole surface down with wire wool between coats. When the second coat is dry, make small pencil marks at 7.5cm (3in) intervals to mark the centres of the stripes.

Make a watery mixture in a soft pink colour, using magenta and cadmium red, and put it into a hand-spray bottle. Using two pieces of scrap card as masks, spray stripes around the frame at each pencil mark – before these are dry, run a brush through each stripe to even it out and continue the stripe on to the sight-edge and the outside edge of the board.

When the stripes are totally dry, rub them down with fine wire wool, revealing the background colour in patches to produce the antiqued effect. Finally, mix the pale ivory shade again, put it into the spray bottle and spray the whole frame lightly.

ASSEMBLY

To make channels to hold the poster, cut six strips of hardboard with a craft knife around 40 to 45 cm (or 16 to 18in) long and 1cm (or ½in) wide and glue them together in pairs. Then cut three 3cm (or 1¼in) wide hardboard strips the same length and glue one of these to each pair of the narrow strips to make L-shaped channels (see the drawing on page 59). When the adhesive is dry, tape the poster behind the aperture on the board, then place the L-shaped channels in position. One is placed at the bottom to support the poster (and, if necessary, to hold the weight of protective glass) and the other two on either side to hold the poster in position. When you are totally satisfied that all three are correct, release the poster and tack the channels in place using 12mm (½in) panel pins and a hammer. The poster can now be slid back into position in the channels.

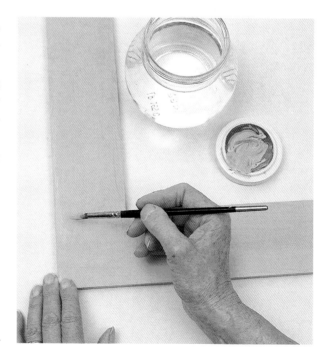

1 With the plywood 'frame' cut to size and with the correct aperture, start the decoration by applying two coats of the background paint colour.

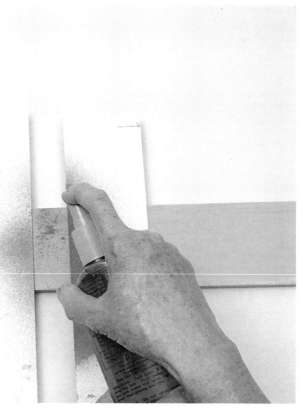

2 An ordinary hand-spray bottle is ideal for spraying stripes in a second colour. Simply mask off the area to be sprayed with two strips of scrap mountboard.

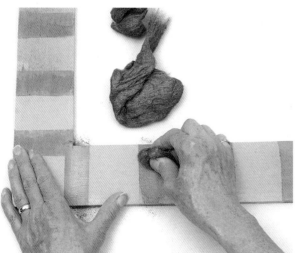

3 Use fine wire wool to rub through the coloured stripes once the paint has dried to produce an 'antique' effect.

4 Make up three L-shaped channels from one wide and two narrow strips of hardboard and position them on the back of the frame to hold the poster in place.

Watercolour

If you paint or collect watercolours and want to frame them, there is only one way to decorate the mount and that is with a washline. Coloured prints can benefit from this treatment as well, and although it takes a little practice, it is effective when it is done and adds a lot to the painting.

You will need

Preparation
- Watercolour
- Plain moulding 2cm (¾in) wide
- Mountboard in ivory
- Basic framing kit
- Basic mount cutting kit

Decoration
- Basic mount decoration kit
- Basic frame decoration kit

Assembly
- Basic assembly kit

PREPARATION

Start by calculating the measurement for the mount because, when a washline is going to be done, the mount must be cut with wider borders than normal. Measure the watercolour itself, allowing a small amount for the part tucked under the mount, then add the width of border to arrive at the final measurement. In this case, the watercolour measured 35 × 31cm (13¾ × 12¼in) and, since it was rather large, I felt that I needed a generous border so I added 9.5cm (3¾in) to the top and sides, and 11.5cm (4½in) to the bottom. This gave a total measurement of 54 × 52 cm (21¼ × 20½in) which is, of course, also the size for the glass and hardboard.

Cut the aperture in the mount and then the four pieces of moulding for the frame allowing ease.

DECORATION

The technique of washlining is described in detail in the *Basic decorative techniques* chapter, but before you embark on this part of the project it would be a good idea to become totally confident with your ruling pen by using it for basic lines on a few mounts, changing the line width and learning how to handle it with the ruler.

For this particular watercolour, I mixed two diluted colours to tone, picking one from the bridge (orangey-red) and one from the water (blue).

1 The colours which you are going to use for the decoration should be matched to the colours of the picture.

2 *The starting point with washlining is to rule the lines in your chosen colours, starting from the inside of the mount and working outwards line by line.*

3 *Making sure your wash colour is mixed ready, start the washline by applying clean water between the two lines and then follow this immediately with the wash itself.*

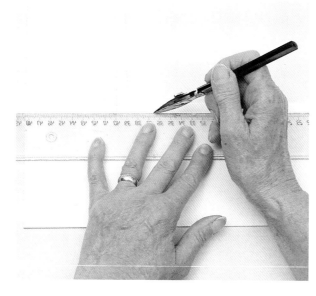

Work out the spacing of your lines using the corner gauge: I decided on 1.5cm for the sight line, 3cm and 5.5cm for the wash and 6.7cm and 7cm for the lead lines – in imperial measurements, I would have used ½in, 2in, 2⅝in and 2¾in. It's always a good idea to experiment with your proposed pattern on a small piece of mountboard and work out where you are going to have the colours when you are introducing more lines.

I decided to make the sides of the wash and the wash itself in the first colour, and the other lines in the second colour, plus a gold line by the side of the wash if I felt it was needed once the washline had been done.

Using the technique described on pages 36 and 37, rule the lines and allow them to dry. Dilute the first colour (here, orangey-red) for the wash and 'paint' the washline with plain clean water. Then, before this has had a chance to dry, apply the wash over the water-covered area between the lines.

To decorate the frame I mixed a thicker mixture of the second colour (blue) with a little pale grey, coating all four pieces of moulding generously and then rubbing off with cotton wool before the paint was quite dry to give a 'washed-out' appearance.

ASSEMBLY

Assemble the frame in the normal way.

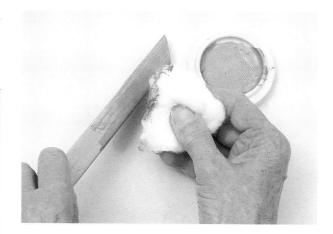

4 *The final part of the decoration is to paint the frame in one of the matching colours. Using cotton wool (or a soft cloth) to rub the paint before it dries gives a 'washed-out' appearance.*

Octagonal frame

Multi-sided frame cutting is always impressive, but all it really needs is stamina! Mitre saws are marked on the base, not only for the conventional 45° angles for a four-sided frame, but also for frames with five, six and eight sides. These multi-sided frames look good with flower paintings, embroideries or portrait photographs and they are always noticed and admired. I recently re-discovered a little machine embroidery that I did years ago and have given it a wide frame and a mount to make it stand out when hung on a wall.

You will need

Preparation
- Embroidery or flower painting
- Wide gold moulding
- Offcut piece of mountboard in ivory
- Circle mount cutter (optional)
- Paper
- Basic framing kit

Assembly
- Glass
- Hardboard
- Basic assembly kit

PREPARATION

Measure the size of your embroidery to work out the size of aperture you need in the mount. I cut my own circular aperture – but unless you have a circle mount cutter, you will probably want to ask a professional picture framer to do this for you. Then consider how much of the mount you want to show – in this case, I decided I did not need more than 2cm (¾in). To this measurement, add the width of the frame rebate (the one I used was rather wide at 1cm) to give the border size – in my case, the aperture was 15.5cm (6in), giving an overall size of 21.5cm (8½in) – and draw a square of this overall size on a piece of paper, which you can then use to work out the dimensions of the octagon – see page 86 for details of how to do this.

Study the base of your mitre saw, and you should see the symbol for an eight-sided frame, and you will find that the saw blade will lock into this position (at 67.5°).

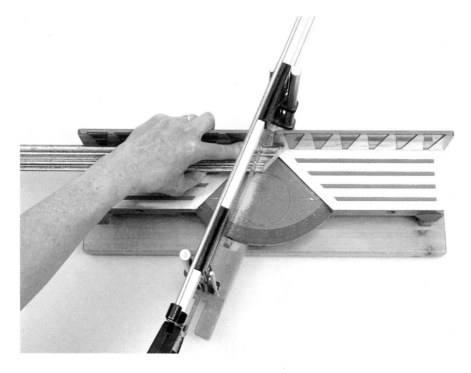

1 Once you have worked out the length of the sides of the octagon, it is cut in the normal way, except that the saw blade is set to the eight-sided frame symbol on the saw body.

Choosing an eight-sided frame means that you have twice as much cutting as usual and it is important when you cut your first multi-sided frame to understand that there is a lot of wastage when you cut, so do allow enough moulding before you start.

Set your saw to the eight-sided symbol and cut the moulding as usual. Then cut angles off the corners of the mountboard to suit the octagonal frame.

DRAWING OUT THE OCTAGON

Take the piece of paper on which you have drawn your square and draw diagonal lines from corner to corner to make a cross. You now need to ascertain how much of each corner needs to be cut off to make an octagon with each of its eight sides the same length. This is done by

measuring half the size of the square – in my case, 10.75cm (4¼in) – out from the centre, parallel with each of the diagonal lines, using the width of the ruler to make your marks either side of the line. Then do the same for each of the other three corners.

In each corner, you will now have two marks, which if you join up, continuing the lines to the edges of the square, will give you an octagon.

The eight sides will all be the same length and it is this measurement that you use for cutting your moulding (for my frame 9cm – 3 ½in). The octagon shape can also be used as a pattern for cutting the mount, the backing and the glass – or, for the glass, you can take the completed frame along to your local glass retailer who will cut the glass to size for you.

HOW TO WORK OUT THE OCTAGON

To work out the size of the octagon, first determine the size of aperture and mount border, then draw a square of this size (L). Draw diagonals and mark half the width of the square at each corner from the centre. Make two marks at each corner and join them up to form the octagon shape.

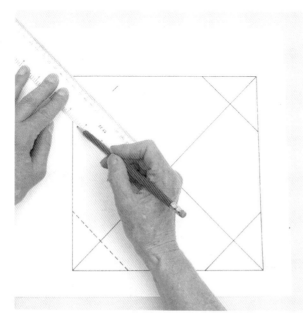

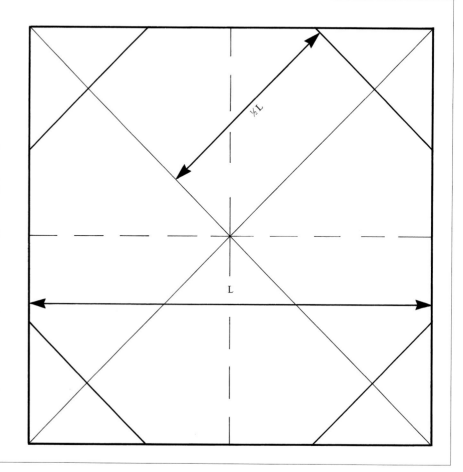

ASSEMBLY

Prepare the band clamp by using all the corner supports provided and fitting the eight pieces of moulding into it. To ensure every joint is glued, I usually take out alternate pieces and apply adhesive to both ends – but, of course, one end of each piece could be coated. The clamp is tightened in the usual way and the resulting frame carefully pinned in the corners when it is dry.

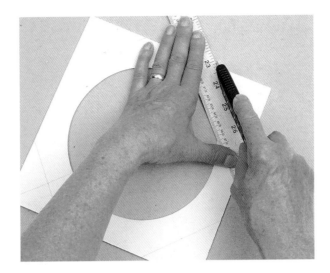

2 The square mount, with its circular aperture, needs to have its corners cut off to suit the size of the octagon.

3 To join an octagonal frame, you will need to use all the corner supports supplied with the band clamp. Before tightening, take out alternate pieces and apply adhesive to both ends before replacing them.

Clown mirror

Adding extensions to a frame is another exciting form of decoration and is particularly suited to mirrors. If they are built on the outside of the frame, they tend to be vulnerable to knocks, but an extension inwards on a frame holds endless possibilities and is protected from damage.

For this 'clown' mirror, I wanted the clown to dominate the design and occupy the bottom of the frame. I decided that a rectangular shape would be best and as I did not want to tie the design to a particular colour scheme, I decided to use four colours and white for the decoration.

You will need

Preparation
- Mirror glass
- Moulding with a flat top profile
- Scraps of plywood the same thickness as the sight-edge of the moulding
- Coping saw
- Basic framing kit

Decoration
- White paper
- Tracing paper
- Self-hardening clay
- Small tins of gloss paint (I chose red, yellow, blue, green and white)
- Small tin of white matt model-makers' paint
- 3 Polystyrene or wooden balls
- Magic finger-lift tape
- Basic frame decoration kit

Assembly
- Basic assembly kit

PREPARATION

Draw the clown design on to a piece of paper and mark out a suitable size of frame with the width of moulding you are using, taking care that most of the clown's body will be on the frame without too many projections going over the mirror – I finally settled for just two projections, one for the clown's arm and one for his knee. Keep this design as your master, tracing it on to tracing paper, then transfer it on to the frame by the old method of scribbling on the back of the lines and drawing over the design on to the frame.

Then trace the extensions on to a small piece of plywood, cut them out with a coping saw and sand any rough edges. You will have to support the extensions

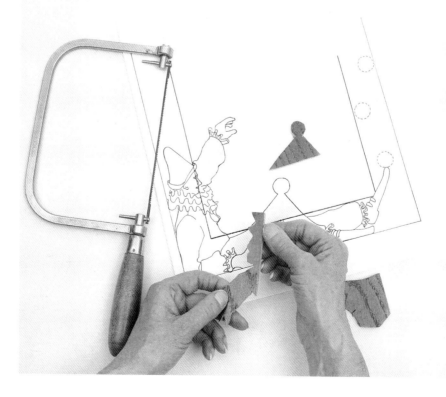

1 Once you have traced the basic clown design on to paper and transferred it to the frame, cut plywood pieces to match the parts of the design extending from the frame.

The basic clown design

KEY

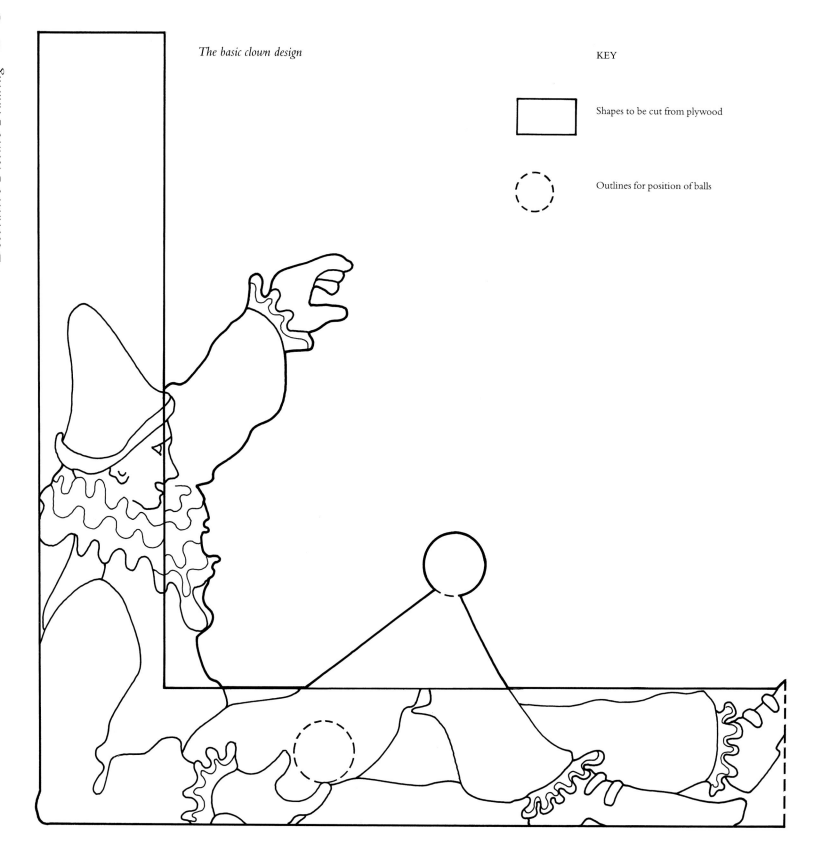

Shapes to be cut from plywood

Outlines for position of balls

Projects

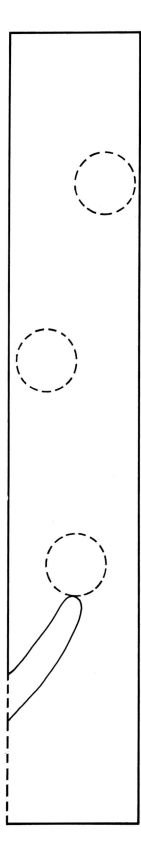

while they are being glued in place – a good way of doing this is with a pile of mountboard offcuts, adjusting the level until the extensions are exactly in position. When you are satisfied, apply adhesive to the edge of the extensions, place them in position and allow them to dry without moving.

I had debated for a while about whether to paint the individual pieces of moulding before making the frame, but finally decided against it on the grounds that the clay is messy to use and also needs sanding when it is dry and this could damage the paintwork.

DECORATION

Once the adhesive is dry, tape the pile of mountboard to the back of the extensions to act as a support while you are modelling the clay. Taking a small piece of clay at a time, start to model the clown in relief, suggesting just

enough form to make him stand out from the frame. Apply a basic coverage and then allow the clay to dry overnight before building up a little more in places such as the brim of the hat, the ruffles round his neck, and his right arm. As you are working, use a cotton bud dipped in water to smooth off areas as this eliminates a lot of subsequent sanding. This type of clay is very good tempered as you can add new damp pieces on to it when it is dry, as well as sanding or even carving it.

In places like the trousers, you need put on very little clay, relying on the curving lines of the paint to give the illusion of form. I also left flat areas on the knee and trousers for the half balls to lie. You can put a little form into the face but again it is best to rely on the painting to give subsequent detail.

When you are happy with the result, the painting can begin. Use finger-lift tape as a mask on the corners of

2 *With the frame extensions glued in place and supported by piles of scrap mountboard, start modelling the clay in the corner. Apply just a small amount of clay at a time and use a cotton bud dipped in water to smooth out each area.*

3 *After leaving the first application of clay to dry overnight, you can carry on building up the clown shape, adding clay where necessary to create the details.*

the moulding and paint each side of the frame individually with three coats of paint, using one of the four colours so that each side is different. Paint carefully around the modelling of the clown and complete the frame before starting to paint the clown itself.

The hat and shirt of the clown are painted in gloss white, and the mask, ruffles and trouser background in matt white. Mix up a pink colour for his neck and hands with matt white and a brush-tip full of red gloss. Paint his shoes two different colours taking care that they contrast with their backgrounds, and paint the laces different colours again. The checks on the trousers can be painted with curving lines to suggest the roundness of the legs using alternate wide and narrow lines in green one way and narrow lines in yellow the other way.

Lastly, enhance his ruffles with edges of blue and red using a very fine brush and, mixing a little blue grey with matt white and a brush-tip full of blue, paint the shadows on his face and in the ruffles.

Cut the polystyrene balls carefully in half using a craft knife (use a fine-toothed saw for wooden balls), paint them in matt white and stick them in place using wood adhesive to give the idea that they are actually being juggled by the clown.

ASSEMBLY

Lay the frame face down on a blanket to protect the surface and secure the mirror and backing board. The final half ball is then stuck on to the mirror with wood adhesive and left to dry overnight.

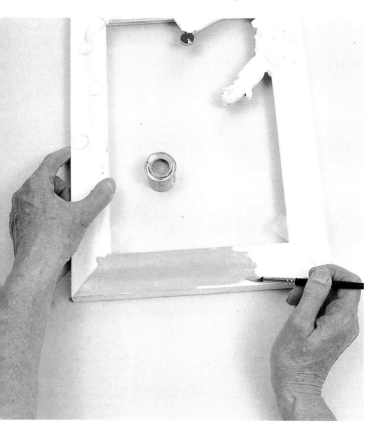

4 Each side of the frame is painted in a different colour. Once three coats have been applied to one side (left), use finger-lift tape to mask it at the corner before painting the next side in another colour (right).

5 *Painting the clown is detailed work, but you can have a lot of fun using the different bright colours. Make sure you use the shaped painted lines to suggest the form of, for example, his trousers.*

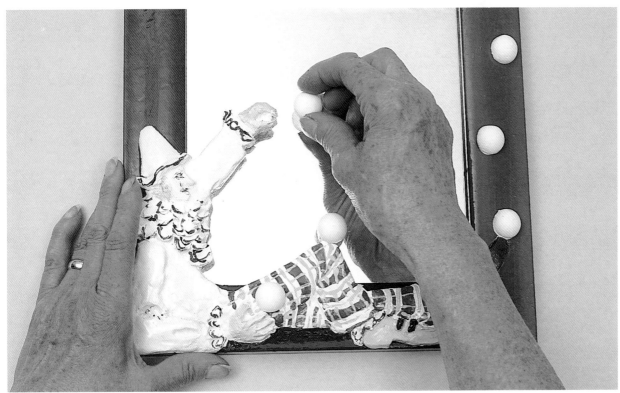

6 *The polystyrene or wooden balls are cut in half, painted white and stuck in place with wood adhesive.*

S u p p l i e r s

Most woodworking tools (including mitre saws) and general supplies can be bought from local hardware shops and DIY stores; picture framing suppliers will have a better selection, but may have a minimum order. Self-hardening modelling clay is available from most art or model shops and finished frames and ready-cut mounts can be bought from art shops or local picture framers. Listed below are companies who can provide a catalogue and supply by mail order.

Chromacolour International Ltd
Cartoon House
11 Grange Mills Weir
London SW12 0NE
0181-675 8422
New artists' paint colours

Homeframe Suppliers Ltd
PO Box 191
Redhill
Surrey RH1 6FW
0181-760 9989
Mitre saws, staple guns, framing clamps, mount cutters, mouldings, backing board, mountboard, tapes, airbrushes, dyes and stains, waxes

Longridge
Grove House
Sherbourne Street
Bembridge
Isle of Wight PO35 5SB
01983-874 121
Mount decorations, corner gauges, mouldings, dyes and stains, waxes, watercolours, paints, brushes and pens

E Ploton (Sundries)
273 Archway Road
London N6 5AA
0181-348 2838
Metal leaf and gilding materials

Tripod Productions
Ely Cottage
Denham
Bury St Edmunds
Suffolk IP29 5EQ
01284-810 387
Band clamps, brad guns/Pushmate, cut mounts, tapes, screw eyes, hooks, cords, corner gauges, dyes and stains, waxes, instructional videos

Index

Acetate film, 59
Adhesives, 10
Aperture
  circular, 84
  cutting, 26–7
  oval, 40
Artist's ruling pen, 16
Assembling frames
  basic kit, 12
  equipment for, 10–13
  technique, 23

Backing boards, 12
  cutting, 23
Band clamp, 10
Beaded frames, miniature, 56–9
Blue and white pottery mosaic, 46
Board, oil painting on, 63–4
Bradawl, 13
Brushes, 15–16

Card, framing, 75–6
Cardboard frames, 25
Ceramic tile adhesive, 48
Child's painting, 60–2
Clamping, 21
Clamps, 10
Clay, modelling, 16
Clown mirror, 88–92
Cord, use for hanging, 13
Corner gauge, 16
Craft knives, 11
Cushion moulding, 12

Decorating frames
  coloured varnish, 31
  dyeing, 30
  equipment for, 15–16
  metal leaf, applying, 32
  paint, using, 32
  techniques, 30–2
  wax, using, 30–1
Decorating mounts
  applied decorations, 33
  cut shapes or buds, 36

masking, 34
rectangular, lining, 33
sponging, 35
spraying, 34
washlining, 36–7
Double mount, cutting, 27
Dyeing frames, 30
Dyes, wood, 15

Equipment
  assembling frames, for, 10–13
  cutting mounts, 13–14
  decorating frames, 15–16
  decorating mounts, 16–17
  making frames, 10–13
Extensions to frame, 69, 88

Fastening devices, 13
Fish, underwater, 69–70
Flat moulding, 12
Flower prints, set of, 66–8
Frames, materials for, 25
Framing techniques, 20–7

Glass, 12
  cleaning, 23
  cutting, 23
Glass cleaner, 13
Glass cutter, 11
Gluing, 21
Gold paint, 32
Gold wax, 31
Greetings card, framing, 75–6
Grouting, 48

Hammers, 10
Hand-held mount cutter, 13
Hanging pictures, 13
Hardboard, cutting, 23
Hockey-stick moulding, 12
Hooks, 13

Kitchen memo board, 46–9
Kitchen poster, 78–80
Knives, 11

Liming wax, 16, 30

Making frames
  basic kit, 11
  equipment for, 10–13
Masking mounts, 34
Measurement, 20
Memo board, 46–9
Metal leaf, 16
  applying, 32
  variations with, 72–4
Miniature beaded frames, 56–9
Mirror
  clown, 88–92
  shell, 43–4
Mitre saw, 10
  using, 20
Modelling clay, 16
Mosaic, 46–9
Mouldings
  clamping, 21
  cushion, 12
  finished, 11
  flat, 12
  gluing, 21
  hockey-stick, 12
  lengths, 11
  rebate, 10
  scoop, 12
  sight-edge, 12
  spoon, 12
  unfinished, 11
Mount cutter, hand-held, 13
Mountboard
  marking, 14
  selection of, 14
  tapes applied to, 17
Mounts
  aperture, cutting, 27
  applied decorations, 33–4
  cut shapes or buds, decorating with,
    36
  cutting to size, 25–6
  decorating, 6, 16–17, 33–7
  double, cutting, 27

equipment for cutting, 13–14
fastening print into, 27
masking, 34
proportions, 25
rectangular, lining, 33
sponging, 35
spraying, 35
washlining, 36–7
Multi-sided frame cutting, 84

Nail punch, 10
Nails, 13

Octagonal frame, 84–7
Oil painting
board, on, 63–4
traditional framing, 6
Old frames
cleaning, 46
corners, strengthening, 25
cutting down, 40
rejuvenating, 25
Old Master print, 50–2
Old photograph, framing, 40–2

Paints, 16–17
frame, decorating, 32
sponging, 35
spraying, 34

washlining, 36–7
Paper, staining, 53
Pens, 16
Pin hammer, 10
Pinning, 21
Plywood, cutting, 56
Plywood frames, 25
Poster, kitchen, 78–80
Practice frame, 20
Print-room effect, 53–4
Prints
flower, 66–8
mount, fastening into, 27
Old Master, 50–2
staining, 53
wall, 53–4
Pushmate, 13

Ready-made frames, 21
Rebate, 10
Rectangular mount, lining, 33
Ruler, 14

Saw, mitre, 10
Scoop moulding, 12
Screw eyes, 13, 23
Self-adhesive decorations, 17
Sepia photograph, framing, 40–2
Shell mirror, 43–4

Softboard, edges, 60
Sponges, 15–16
Sponging, 35
Spoon moulding, 12
Spraying, 35
Straight-edge, 14

Tapes
back of pictures, for, 13, 23
double mounts, fastening, 14
face of mountboard, applied to, 17

Underwater fish, 69–70

Varnish, coloured, 31

Washlining, 36–7
Watercolour
framing, 81–2
traditional framing, 6
Waxes, 16
gold, 31
using, 30–1
Wire, use for hanging, 13
Wire wool, using, 25
Wood adhesives, 10
Wood-coloured wax, 16
Wood dyes, 15

Index

ACKNOWLEDGEMENTS
I would like to thank William for all his help, Sibile for her photocopying skills and Sarah for her paintings.